Hunting the Nazarene

The Second Resurrection of Christ

T0154602

Hunting the Nazarene

The Second Resurrection of Christ

John Koerner

Winchester, UK
Washington, USA

First published by Chronos Books, 2016
Chronos Books is an imprint of John Hunt Publishing Ltd., Laurel House, Station Approach,
Alresford, Hants, SO24 9JH, UK
office1@jhpbooks.net
www.johnhuntpublishing.com

For distributor details and how to order please visit the 'Ordering' section on our website.

ISBN: 978 1 78535 316 1
Library of Congress Control Number: 2015954379

A CIP catalogue record for this book is available from the British Library.

Design: Lee Nash

Printed and bound in the USA by Edwards Brothers Malloy

We operate a distinctive and ethical publishing philosophy in all
areas of our business, from our global network of authors to
production and worldwide distribution.

CONTENTS

Introduction: The Missing Chapter

Qui locutus est per sanctos prophetas[1]

As a professor of American History for the past decade it has disturbed me that mainstream historians are afraid of God. Not that they fear His wrath, but in the sense that our history textbooks have no appreciation of how much religion has influenced people's lives and actions throughout history. Our separation of church and state has separated God from history. Teaching history should never be about making anyone a believer in a specific faith, nor should it ignore how faith has shaped the past. One of the earliest flags in U.S. history was boldly emblazoned with the words "Appeal to Heaven." Lincoln's second inaugural address, perhaps his finest speech, would be devoid of most of its meaning if God was removed from it. Our very currency has been placed within the trust of God Himself, meant to be a stark contrast with our godless communist adversaries in the Cold War. Presidents from both major parties can scarcely end a speech without asking God to bless America. The United States has seen two Great Awakenings in the United States, and the birth of two of the fastest growing religions on earth, Scientology and Mormonism, and yet we are still afraid to teach about God with a fact-based, academic approach. This is how the Jesus of history should be examined. Facts are stubborn things, John Adams was fond of saying, and the historical Jesus needs to be reexamined in this light.

My early work as an author and a historian took me into the field of religious mysteries. In examining the life and miracles of Father Nelson Baker, and Father Patrick Power, I investigated miracles through the template of science and evidence, not faith and belief. I have come to the conclusion that science and religion do not have to be bitter enemies. They can easily coexist. In fact, science can be used as a template to prove the existence of the miraculous. The Catholic Church does this with teams of scientists and historians who prove scientific miracles needed for the canonization process. My books on Baker and Power include a number of miracles that by definition cannot be explained by science. It is with this logical approach informed by these years of research that we begin the investigation into the probability that Jesus of Nazareth rose from the dead a second time.

Where is the evidence for this? As we will see, the Gospel of John all but gives away this centuries old secret by leaving a huge narrative gap between chapter 20 and chapter 21, the conclusion of the fourth gospel. Chapter 20 is filled with hope and promise as Christ has returned from the dead and has dramatically called his apostles to action, convincing even the most skeptical of all the believers. Then suddenly, and with stunning immediacy, the apostles have splintered. Within days, the corps leadership group has inexplicably and completely given up, returning to a life that their master had forbidden them to return to. Why would the apostles so readily break up, and then give up, when they had just been rejuvenated by the return of Christ? The only other time this happens in the gospels is when Jesus was crucified. That sent them into despair and into hiding. The conclusion that we are going to reach in this book is that the apostles must have found out that the Son of Man had been executed again by the Romans. This behavior mirrors exactly what they did the first time that Christ died. For a second time, led by Peter, they deliberately chose to end their commitment to Christ in a profound display of utter apostasy. The only factor that could cause such damage to the 11, to end their commitment to Jesus would be if they believed He was dead again. In fact, I will argue that Christ willing submitted Himself to this for some very logical reasons. I admit that this premise will be difficult for many to accept, but ask yourself if billions of people throughout history have believed that Jesus of Nazareth rose from the dead once, why would it not be possible for Him to do so a second time?

In order to prove this, I will demonstrate first that the apostles were ready, willing, and able to begin their missionary work by the end of chapter 20, that Pentecost should have begun then, not later in the Acts of the Apostles. Once that is established, we will make the case for rampant apostasy in chapter 21, which would make little sense if the 11 believed their leader was still walking the earth. Another part of this process will be to dispel the absurd notion that chapter 21 was added on by a different author who was not St. John. As we will see the style is distinctly that of the beloved apostle.

Finally, this book will conclude with a brief fictional account of the last days of Jesus on this earth, based off the evidence presented in the first part of the book. This will allow us to get a better sense of how these events may have transpired 2,000 years ago.

Throughout this book you will find a pursuit of the truth. I have designed this work to be watertight against any potential holes in my argumentation. I have tried to think of every conceivable way that the thesis of this book might be attacked or undermined because I assume many will ignore it, or simply dismiss it outright. However, for those truth seekers with an open mind you will find nothing but logic and evidence within these pages. I have put myself in the position of the skeptic who would question every word. I am confident in my approach here that any argument made against my thesis can be answered with facts, evidence, and logic. My own personal journey while writing this book has taken me along paths I never suspected when I first began this manuscript. All of those wise and careful influences who may have been guiding me along the way in this world or beyond, I thank you for your patience and faith in me. I have nothing but love and respect for you and I pray that I have made you proud with all that follows.

John Koerner
February 2015

Part One

The Second Resurrection of Christ

Chapter One

Confronting Pilate

The Importance of Judas

Et crucifixus est pro nobis sub Pontio Pilato et sepultus est.[2]

It is historically irresponsible to regard Judas Iscariot as merely the traitor who handed over the messiah to certain death. Modern day thinking regards him more as a trusted middle man, a confidant whom the Son of Man could rely upon to coordinate the crucifixion as according to what had been prophesied in Holy Scripture. Author William Klassen in his book *Judas: Betrayer or Friend of Jesus* contends that Judas did not betray Jesus at all. Klassen found that the word "betrayal," found throughout all of the English versions of the Bible, is a misinterpretation of the Greek word "paradidomi," which translates to "handed over."[3] The author argues that Judas was deliberately slandered throughout history to provide an easy scapegoat for humanity's collective guilt about the crucifixion.[4]

When Jesus rose from the dead, it must have been quite devastating to Him to come to terms with the fact that Judas had died with his king. One has to wonder if Jesus foresaw this end for perhaps his closest friend. Christ displayed enormous compassion toward Judas at the Last Supper saying "woe to that man by whom the Son of Man is betrayed. It would be better for that man if he had never been born"[5] (Matthew 26: 24). Notice that Jesus did not say "it would be better if that man had never been born."

Judas had to be born to help Jesus bring His life to an end on His own terms, with the help of His most reliable apostle. It is likely that the other 11 men would refuse to allow Jesus to be captured by the Romans or the Jews. They would be unable to understand how this could be part of God's plan. Judas was the only one Christ could count on to do what had to be done, according to the will of the Master. Judas had been trusted to be the group's treasurer, was most likely the best educated member of the group, and a fierce defender of Jesus.[6]

When Judas killed himself he left an indelible hole in the power structure of the 12 apostles. Did his suicide condemn Judas to hell? Did Jesus bring Judas out of hell when He descended there after His crucifixion? Given the vacillating nature of Peter, Judas was in many ways the de facto leader. Within 24 hours, the two most important members of this group of 13 were dead. The remaining 11 were understandably frightened for their lives, and lacking strong leadership to keep them moving forward to preach Jesus' message.

One factor that may have persuaded Christ to consider submitting Himself to further degradation was the loss of this key figure in the 12 apostles. Perhaps it seemed to Jesus that at least for this group the resurrection was still not enough to convince them of the need to become messengers of Christ. The effect of the loss of Judas was something that Christ increasingly had to deal with in the weeks after his return. Perhaps one reason Jesus had to repeatedly make appearances to His followers was to instill faith in them that was sorely lacking, in part because of the loss of Judas. A second resurrection would be meant for only the apostles to know about, that Jesus could return at any time, accounting for the numerous times the apostles talk about his coming again in the latter half of the New Testament. The first resurrection was not enough to convince the apostles to take up their own cross for Him. He needed to test their faith a second time to prepare them for the difficulties ahead.

A renewed threat

After Jesus rose from the dead and spent 40 days walking the earth, this incredible news began to spread that He had returned among 12 different groups of people.7 St. Paul in his first letter to the Corinthians almost offhandedly mentions that Jesus "appeared to more than five hundred brothers at once." St. Paul then added, likely so as to prove his knowledge of this, that most of these witnesses "are still living, though some have fallen asleep"8 (1 Corinthians 15:6).

It is counterintuitive to imagine that reports of these dramatic events would not have spread to Pontius Pilate. In fact, Matthew reports that when the Sanhedrin got word of Jesus' resurrection from the guards who witnessed it, they thought immediately that Pilate might find out about this too[9] (Matthew 28:14). And from that point it would have been in Pilate's best interest to investigate the matter, especially given the fact that according to his wife he would be eternally damned for his recent actions. The high priests had even told Pilate that if the resurrection did turn out to be true, or if the apostles made it look like Jesus rose from the dead by stealing His body, "this last impostor would be worse than the first,"[10] (Matthew 28: 64) as they put it. It would be devastating for those who executed Jesus if the story came out (real or not) that He had risen from the dead. This would undermine the authority, credibility, and power of the Sanhedrin and Pilate. This in fact was why the Jews asked Pilate for more guards at the tomb. This shows that if necessary they would be ready to kill Him again. They wanted to take no chances. Perhaps that is why Joseph of Arimathea, a member of the Sanhedrin, was allowed to take the body and place it in his tomb. He could be relied upon to allow the area around the tomb to be placed under what amounted to martial law. There were probably orders to kill anyone who attempted to move the body, or kill Jesus if He came out of that tomb. We can easily conclude based on logic and by their own actions that the Jews and Pilate would not hesitate to execute Christ a second time if they had to. Letting Him live would undermine their authority and credibility.

One also has to suspect that Pilate would consider executing the remaining 11 apostles for crimes against the state, and the Sanhedrin would feel the same way about this, seeking to erase this Man from history by killing His followers too. In fact, it would go against Pilate's behavioral pattern to not target the remaining 11 apostles. This man had a well-earned reputation for maintaining order with an iron fist. In 26 A.D. the Roman Emperor Tiberius appointed Pontius Pilate prefect of the Roman provinces of Judaea, Samaria, and Idumaea. He was given the authority of supreme judge, as well as keeper of law and order which he accomplished through brute force.[11] Ancient Jewish historian Philo noted that if the Roman emperor sent a delegation to investigate Pilate, "they would also expose the rest of his conduct as governor by stating in full the briberies, the insults, the robberies, the outrages and wanton injuries, the executions without trial constantly repeated, the ceaseless and supremely grievous cruelty."[12] For example, Jewish historian Josephus recorded an incident where Pilate placed scores of soldiers hidden within a group of protesting Jews who were then ordered to randomly pummel and kill them to quell unrest.[13] In 36 A.D., three years after the crucifixion of Jesus, Pilate ordered the massacre of a group of Samaritans on Mt. Gerizim. These Jews believed in the ancient sanctity of this mountain and had gathered there to look at vessels which Moses allegedly made for the Tabernacle.[14]

Jesus would have known about this threat. He was a practical and intelligent leader, and was keenly aware that His message would not live on unless these 11 men found a way to spread it freely. Therefore, if Pilate and the Sanhedrin would seemingly want the apostles dead so they could not spread the story of Jesus, thereby showing how wrong the Jews and Romans were to execute Him, this leads us to a logical question to ask. How is it then that in the Acts of the Apostles, Peter is able to openly give speeches about Christ in the streets of Jerusalem, and hold what amount to recruitment rallies right under the nose of Pilate and the Sanhedrin without being assassinated immediately? St. Luke reports that at Pentecost after Peter stood up and gave a rousing address to the people of Israel "about 3,000 people were added that day"[15] (Acts 2:41). His lengthy speech chronicled in chapter 2 of the Acts of Apostles must have lasted nearly an hour right under the nose of Roman authorities. Peter continued making his public proclamations in chapter 3, converting another 5,000 until he got arrested by the Jews. Yet when the apostles were taken in front of the Sanhedrin, St. Luke notes that "after threatening them further, they released them, finding no way to punish them..."[16] (Acts 4:21). Luke also says that after St. Stephen was martyred, many others began to be rounded up and killed all throughout Jerusalem and the countryside, but curiously "except the apostles" [17] (Acts 8:1). How did John live long past the resurrection, even making a visit with Peter to Samaria to bless some new converts there?[18] How in fact did the four gospels even get the chance to see the light of day?

Jesus would have recognized these practical problems facing his newly forming church. I would contend that after several weeks speaking with the apostles, (and probably His mother too), seeing their fear, and recognizing this practical problem, Christ decided to stage a dramatic confrontation with Pilate, the Sanhedrin, or perhaps both of them. This would not be done as an arrogant slap in the face. The purpose of this would be to allow Himself to be captured again to show these key leaders His divine power firsthand so that they would leave his apostles alone, and allow them to preach.

Keep in mind this is exactly what Jesus did with Saul, who was a key threat to the existence of His newly forming church. "Saul, meanwhile, was trying to destroy the church; entering house after house and dragging out men and women, he handed them over for imprisonment"[19] (Acts 8: 3). Jesus decided to demonstrate to Saul a dramatic display of divine power meant to shock and awe this man into a believer. This appearance happened after the Ascension, making it even more supernaturally impressive, given the fact that the flesh and blood of Jesus was no longer on this earth. On his way to Damascus to continue his reign of terror Saul fell to the ground when he saw a light from the sky that flashed all around him, leaving him blind for three days[20] (Acts 9). The voice of Jesus told him to stop the persecutions, which of course he did, and then went on to become one of the most important leaders in Catholic history.

A similar display of divine power in front of the Sanhedrin and Pilate could have this same effect. If Jesus saw that Saul was a threat, and we can logically conclude that Pilate and the Sanhedrin were at least an equal if not greater threat, it therefore makes absolutely no sense from a logical standpoint that He would do nothing to address this issue because He took direct action when it came to Saul. A second resurrection witnessed by these men could have a similar effect. It would serve two practical purposes for Christ that the first one seemingly was not intended for. The first crucifixion and resurrection was for all of mankind to save the world from our sins. Despite this, the apostles were still fearful of their lives and lacked leadership without Jesus and Judas. Additionally, there was the threat of assassination from the Sanhedrin and Pontius Pilate. This would end any hope that the church could continue. Perhaps it is no coincidence then that despite the fact that Pilate lived until 39 A.D.[21] and stayed in power several years after Jesus' crucifixion, there is not one word about him in the Acts of the Apostles. There is no recorded attempt by Pilate in that pivotal book to stamp out the early church, despite the fact that it would be in his interest to do so. Pilate would want to maintain order, and erase the memory of this messiah that he had mistakenly put to death, and yet there is no recorded evidence of him doing anything of the kind.

We should also examine the role that Pilate's wife, Claudia played in this. In Matthew 27:19, Pilate's wife warns her husband through a messenger not to execute the innocent man who stood before him. She knew through a dream that Jesus was being wrongly accused. At that moment Jesus would have recognized in Claudia a potential friend. If Jesus was going to make the decision to rise from the dead a second time in a grand display of divine power in front of Pilate, he would have known that Claudia would be a key ally to keep Pilate from persecuting His church. In fact, it is likely that Claudia later became a Christian and perhaps was the Claudia that Paul of all people mentions in his second letter to Timothy. In fact, she was later canonized by the Greek Orthodox Church. Claudia was the granddaughter of Emperor Augustus.[22] Such a powerful supporter would be very appealing to Jesus, not to mention the fact that Christ wanted women to play a key role in the early church as evidenced by His special relationship with Mary Magdalene. Jesus would have known, that like with Saul, a firsthand display of divine power in front of Claudia and Pilate would be enough to convince the Romans to stay away, and put in the minds of the apostles that He could return at any time to help them through this difficult time. Jesus would deliberately let it be known that He was captured a second time to test the faith of His apostles and ensure that they would not be assassinated. It is likely that He would turn to a specific person to do this: John.

The role of the beloved disciple

As we are going to see later, a second resurrection of Christ would fit perfectly between chapter 20 and chapter 21 of the Gospel of John. I believe John put all the clues there for us to figure this out centuries later. One possibility is that a second resurrection was not meant for the public to know about so John either deliberately left this out of his gospel, or it was removed by the Catholic Church. It would be too difficult to convince non believers of a second resurrection, let alone a first one. It was probably a dramatic specific event in front of the Sanhedrin or the Romans for the reasons stated above. Christ likely discussed this with His mother and John who were living together, that something dramatic needed to be done to keep the apostles safe and test their faith to keep them strong. John would be trusted to hand over Christ to the Romans at a specific time and place. Jesus would count on John's young age as a deterrent that would keep the Romans from killing him. One possible scenario is that this second display of divine power would be done directly in front of John who had already seen his savior die once, so he knew what to expect. He also knew what would be expected of him. He would witness this, but never record it in his gospel. Perhaps Jesus even told him to keep this a secret.

The other possibility is that Jesus had John turn him over to the authorities a second time and then, not witness Jesus' second death, and then report this back to the apostles as another test of their faith. Christ may not have told John of His true intentions, only to have faith. The beloved disciple would then report this horrible news to Peter that Jesus had been captured again. Such an event however is the only logical narrative bridge we can make between chapter 20 and chapter 21 of his gospel. Something unspoken and unwritten goes horribly wrong between those two chapters, something of such magnitude that it splintered the entire power structure in the high command of the apostle leadership corp. The only logical conclusion we can make then is that the apostles must have assumed their leader had been captured and killed again, reported to them by John somewhere between the days that expire between chapter 20 and chapter 21 of the Gospel of John. When Jesus submitted Himself to this second round of suffering, He likely planned to die and come back to life within sight of Pontius Pilate and the Jews, and then make a final reappearance to His friends. It is time to understand what truly happened in those mysterious forty days after Jesus came out of that tomb. His work was only just beginning. A new set of challenges lay ahead. Convincing the apostles to carry on His work, and making sure they did not get assassinated, were two immediate concerns that had to be addressed before the Ascension. Offering Himself up for more suffering could solve both of these problems.

Chapter Two

The Missing Pentecost

Jesus commissions the apostles

Et resurrexit tertia die[23]

There is absolutely no reason why the Acts of the Apostles should not begin after chapter 20 of the Gospel of John. As we will demonstrate in this section, everything that was needed to begin teaching the good news is in place when the door is closed on chapter 20. Jesus has dramatically returned from the dead, repeatedly visited His disciples, and has even convinced the most skeptical of all His followers, doubting Thomas. The corps group is energized, rejuvenated, and hopeful again. It is time to take it to the streets, and bring in the thousands of followers that Pentecost, the birthday of the church, converted on that miraculous day.

Christ first appeared to Mary Magdalene, perhaps the most efficient way to spread the news that He had returned. He likely knew that since His death she had been in utter despair. Having seen Him resurrected she would not be able to contain her joy. It would be obvious to anyone that she was not lying with such a marked difference in her behavior. Christ would count on the fact that she would tell this news to the apostles, to test their faith. In fact, John reports that is exactly what she did, saying that she "went and announced to the disciples, 'I have seen the Lord,' and what he told her"[24] (John 20:18).

Jesus followed this up with two visits to the apostles. The first was a dramatic entry into their secret hiding place where they had stayed "for fear of the Jews"[25] (John 20:19). Importantly, Christ gave these men the gift of the Holy Spirit during this first visit. This was the same gift they received at Pentecost in chapter

15

two of the Acts of the Apostles, the difference though, was that in the Acts of the Apostles, Christ was not present during that visitation of the Holy Spirit. The visit of the Holy Spirit was much more dramatic in the Gospel of John because it took place within the presence of Christ. Two members of the Holy Trinity were present on earth for perhaps the first time in human history. Logically we must conclude that this would be supernaturally impressive to these fishermen. Jesus is commissioning the disciples at this moment to be priests. He even invoked the first member of the Trinity in some of most powerful words in this gospel. "Peace be with you. As my Father has sent me, so I send you"[26] (John 20: 21). Jesus was saying that the apostles are ready to be sent into the world with the mandate of God the Father Himself. The next step was for the Son of Man to invest within these men the grace and power of the Holy Spirit to give them the strength and courage to spread His message. "And when He had said this, He breathed on them and said to them, 'Receive the Holy Spirit. Whose sins you forgive are forgiven them, and whose sins you retain are retained'"[27] (John 20:22-23).

Theologian Sir Edwyn Hoskyns sees this event as no less than as "the apostolic commission of the disciples," he writes in his landmark work *The Fourth Gospel*. At this moment they are made "Apostles of the Son of God...but in order that they may be made adequate for their work, they must be transformed and recreated by the insufflations of the Holy Spirit...Inspired with divine authority, and invested with the power of the Father, Son, and Holy Spirit, the disciples are enabled to undertake the contest with sin."[28] St. Thomas Aquinas says of this scene in the gospel that Jesus "charges the apostles with their ministry: first, he grants them the bond of peace; secondly, he charges them, as the Father has sent me...This shows that he is the intermediary between us and God," said Aquinas. "This was a source of strength for the disciples: for they recognized the authority of Christ, and knew that he was sending them by divine authority…Jesus makes them adequate for their task by giving them the Holy Spirit."[29]

This has all the markings of Pentecost. The apostles have received the Holy Spirit and have witnessed firsthand that their messiah has been raised from the dead. That very moment they should be filled with such unfettered rejoicing that nothing less than death could stop them from telling this news, like Mary Magdalene. Jesus has specifically said with His words and shown with His hands that they have the backing of no less than all three parts of the Holy Trinity itself. By His own words He is "sending" them into the world with peace in their hearts. He is saying now is the time to go forth, like He had been sent by His Father.

And yet even after this visit, Jesus still feels the need to visit these men again, to further reassure them about the importance of the work ahead. Perhaps it was in these intervening days when the apostles still had not taken it to the streets that He decided on the need for a second resurrection. This was a week later and yet the apostles were still locked inside their secret headquarters, still unwilling to begin the mission. Jesus again brings the gift of peace to the apostles at this second visit, like He did the first time. This peace is meant to still their fear, and end any rancor that may have existed within the ranks of the apostles about what to do next. The peace He brings is another tool to use to begin their mission of preaching His message in the streets.

This second visit to the apostles in the Gospel of John is also meant to remove any doubt that Jesus has risen from the dead. Thomas, also called Didymus, was not present during the first visitation of Christ after His resurrection. Known allegorically as "doubting Thomas," he was apparently the most cynical and skeptical of the group. John uses this passage in his gospel to imply that if Thomas could be convinced that Jesus was real, then anyone could. If Thomas believed it then, it must be true because he said, "unless I see the mark of the nails in his hands and put my finger into the nailmarks and put my hand into His side, I will not believe"[30] (John 20: 25). Jesus allowed Thomas to put his hands on Him to feel all the wounds from His crucifixion. Thomas answered famously, "My Lord and My God!"[31] (John 20: 28).

At this point in the Bible, the Acts of the Apostles should commence. They have been given two chances to answer their life calling, their very reason for being born. And yet they hesitate. A week passed and they did nothing. Christ came again to remove any doubt a second time. You could imagine His growing frustration with these men. Under the divine guidance of the Holy Spirit these 11 elect should be ready to start preaching, forgiving sins, performing miracles, getting recruits, and testifying to the historical truth of the bodily resurrection of Jesus of Nazareth which they have seen with their eyes, and felt with their hands. Peter's dramatic speech in the streets of Jerusalem should logically be the next event in the Bible. The 8,000 converts that the apostles recruit in the first few days of the church, as we noted above, should be how this story continues. And yet, as we will see next, chapter 21 marks a massive deviation from this course. Instead of the birthday of Catholicism happening next, the church is all but dead in chapter 21. The scene was very similar to late 1776 when the British had taken Philadelphia, New York City, and occupied many loyalist towns throughout the 13 colonies. Washington's barefoot, starving army was deserting him on a daily basis. Thomas Paine would say that "these were the times that tried men's souls,"[32] when most had given up on the cause of independence, and had gone back home. The apostles felt the same way in chapter 21. Four members of the group splintered away from the rest to return to their families, while the remaining seven reverted to their careers as fishermen. With no explanation from John, these 11 men had completely given up.

Proving John's authorship

However, before we can prove this utter apostasy, we need to dispel the notion that chapter 21 was added on later by a different author, something that John himself seems to foresee at the end of the chapter by recounting an odd scene with Jesus. Peter seems jealous of the special relationship between John and Jesus. Christ sharply snaps at Peter for inquiring about John, saying to him, "What concern is it of yours?"[33] (John 21:22). This heated encounter seems to be yet another way that John was trying to prove that he was a firsthand, privileged witness to these events. "It is this disciple who testifies to these things and has written them, and we know that his testimony is true"[34] (John 21:24). John probably knew that the odd nature of chapter 21 would be questioned by many of his readers so he wanted to make it absolutely clear that he himself was a witness to these dramatic events.

We can also point out that if we want to briefly delve into the area of belief and not logic, which I am reluctant to do, according to the Catholic Church the Bible is divinely inspired by the Holy Spirit "who has spoken through the prophets." Therefore it does not matter who authored chapter 21 because by definition the Church would argue that God wanted it put there and directed that it be put there through the divine inspiration of the Holy Spirit, no matter who the actual author was. Fortunately, we do not need to go down this path. Logic can get us to the same result that John authored this chapter, just like the rest of the gospel.

Before we prove that John authored chapter 21, I would be remiss if I did not briefly establish that St. John is in fact the author of the fourth gospel. Although this is not necessary to prove the thesis of this book, it does help to know beyond any doubt that we are dealing with an author who was a firsthand witness to these events and therefore can be trusted to give us at least his version of events. Much has been written to establish his authorship and there is no need to laboriously go over all of the arguments, however I will take us through the salient points that most historians have used to give John his proper credit, as it were. Then we will deal with chapter 21 and prove his authorship of that epilogue to the fourth gospel.

Perhaps the most thorough and convincing work done by any author that I have come across that deals with this material is the work of historian and theologian Michal Elizabeth Hunt. She has spent 30 years researching and reflecting on sacred scripture and founded the Agape Bible Study group. Here is a brief summary of her arguments.

Many bible critics have said that John was too wrathful and emotional to write such a book filled with themes of love based on the label Jesus gave to him and his brother as "Sons of Thunder." Hunt counters that point by saying that by the time John wrote the book he would have surely outgrown his impetuous youth because by then he was a fully grown older man serving as Bishop of Ephesus.

Another argument is that the author must have come from Greek culture because of the Hellenistic thought and concepts which were not found in Jewish literature of the first century in Israel. Hunt says that this is simply not true. The Dead Sea Scrolls proved that Greek influences were widespread in Jewish literature during that time period. Moreover, every village in the Holy Land would likely have taught every young boy Greek which was the international language of commerce.

A third argument against the authorship of the beloved apostle is that an uneducated fisherman from Galilee could never write such a work. Hunt proves that this family was nothing but poor. James and John along with their father Zebedee were partners with Peter and Andrew. The scale of their operation was large enough so that they could hire helpers, own several boats, and start and stop work when they pleased. The scale and location of Peter's house when excavated at Capernaum proved that these were men of considerable means. "I do not know of any serious scholar who believes Peter, Andrew, and Zebedee & sons were poor," says Hunt. She also points out that every synagogue would teach the boys of the village Hebrew, Aramaic, and Greek. "The

Greek of the fourth gospel is the simplest of the New Testament Greek texts," she writes, "precisely what one might expect from a man who learned Greek as a second language."

A fourth argument is that John does not name himself in the gospel but only calls himself "the beloved disciple." Hunt points out that this is an act of humility, plus there would be no reason to identify himself to his readers who already knew who he was. Moreover, none of the other gospel writers identify themselves either.

Also, we can rather easily prove that the "beloved disciple" was in fact St. John. "The author accurately portrays Old Covenant customs, religious traditions, and the fine points of legal regulations that were unique to Israel as God's holy covenant people," says Hunt. "The inspired writer of this Gospel is knowledgeable about the different sects of 1st century Judaism and is especially knowledgeable about the geography and topography of what was the Roman dominated province of Judea and the city of Jerusalem, identifying and correctly describing sites that were not rediscovered in Jerusalem until the late 1800s. All these qualifications fit John the Apostle." Hunt further clarifies this point in her analysis by adding the following points.

But how do we know which of the Apostles is "the one Jesus loved"? The Synoptic Gospels identify 3 Apostles that Jesus singled out on important occasions. These were Peter, to whom Jesus gave the "keys of the kingdom," James, the son of Zebedee, and James' younger brother, the Apostle John. It was to this trinity of Apostles that Jesus chose to reveal Himself in His glory on the Mt. of Transfiguration (Matthew 17:1-2; Mark 9:2-8; Luke 9:28-36). We can narrow down the identity of the inspired writer of the fourth Gospel to one of these 3 men and, by eliminating the other 2, we can come to one final name.

The "beloved disciple" who authors the fourth Gospel cannot be Peter because the fourth Gospel records that on several occasions Peter was accompanied by the "beloved disciple" (John 20:2; 21:20). James Zebedee is eliminated as a candidate for the "beloved disciple" by the fact that he was the first Apostle to be martyred (circa 42AD). We have an accurate date for his martyrdom not only from Christian sources (Acts 12:2, etc.) but also from Jewish accounts. This fact eliminates James because the fourth Gospel was written at least 25 years after his death. That only leaves John, son of Zebedee, as the "beloved disciple."[35]

Hunt concludes her study by demonstrating that numerous church leaders for hundreds of years testified to the divine authorship of St. John including figures such as St. Clement of Alexandria, and St. Theophilus, bishop of Antioch.[36]

Having established that John was the author of the fourth gospel, let us prove that he wrote chapter 21 as well, and that it was not added on by a different author. First of all, we know that chapter 21 appears in all manuscripts of the Gospel of John. It has never been missing from it in any of even the earliest editions of the Bible, which if missing would indicate the later addition by another author.[37]

Another point to make is that two other works by John the Apostle have an epilogue, like chapter 21. This seems to be the writing style of the beloved apostle, to have a second ending to complement the first. The first letter of John includes a prayer for sinners as a second ending to that sacred missive. The second and third letters of John are far too short to be able to have or need an epilogue, but the same does not go for the Book of Revelation, whose authorship is also attributed to John. The final book of the Bible ends with another Johannine type epilogue where the author states, "it is I, John, who heard and saw these things, and when I heard and saw them I fell down to worship at the feet of the angel who showed them to me"[38] (Revelation 22:8). So therefore if the Gospel of John was missing such an epilogue like chapter 21 it would indicate authorship from a different source. In other words, the very unique nature of that chapter helps us prove that it came from John, and not another source.

The language of chapter 21 is also similar to the rest of the gospel. John uses the phrase "the disciple whom Jesus loved" to identify himself in chapter 21 two times in verse 7 and verse 20. This is the same way he identified himself earlier in the Gospel of John 13:23[39], John 19:26[40], and John 20:2.[41] He also calls himself that name again five times in the Book of Revelation, providing more ties to that phraseology from chapter 21.[42]

The dialogue that John has in chapter 21 is also the same as the rest of the gospel in many specific ways. Having listened to Jesus speak so often, the beloved disciple knows that when the Lord is about to say something important He says "Amen, amen, I say to you" like He does in the 18th verse of chapter 21. "Amen, amen, I say to when you were younger you used to dress and go where you wanted, but when you grow old, you will stretch out your hands, and someone else will dress you, and lead you where you do not want to go"[43] (John 21:18).

John reports Jesus saying this phrase many times throughout his gospel. "Amen, amen, I say to you, everyone who commits sin is a slave of sin"[44] (John 8:34). "Amen, amen, I say to you whoever does not enter a sheepfold through the gate but climbs over elsewhere is a thief and a robber"[45] (John 10:1). "Amen, amen, I say to you, unless a grain of wheat falls to the ground and dies, it remains just a grain of wheat, but if it dies it produces much fruit"[46] (John 12:24). This phrase obviously connects chapter 21 with the rest of the gospel.

"The language is throughout (chapter 21) Johannine,"[47] says Hoskyns. He cites many other words and phrases from chapter 21 that appear earlier in the gospel, in John 1, or in the Book of Revelation. For example, the phrase "after this," which begins chapter 21 is also how John started chapters 5, 6, and 7. The word "again" from John 21:1 refers back to John 20:19, and 26; while "the sea" is from John 6:16. Hoskyns also points out that the Greek word for "catch" in chapter 21 is used six other times in the fourth gospel, but nowhere in the other three gospels. "The charcoal fire" was mentioned in John 18:18, while the apostles' hesitation to question Jesus is similar to John 4:27, and John 16:23. The failure to recognize Jesus also happened in John 20:14, and the Eucharistic words hearken back to John 6:11.

"Thomas and Nathanael are especially Johannine characters," says Hoskyns. "Cana is a Johannine place-name...The relation between the beloved disciple and Peter recalls John 20: 2-8, where the perception of the former and the impetuosity of the latter are emphasized. It is almost impossible," Hoskyns concludes, "to attribute the subtle similarity of style to conscious imitation."[48] The late theologian Raymond E. Brown, a professor at Union Theological Seminary, looked into this question as well and found that among other scholars who share the viewpoint that no one else but John could have authored chapter 21 "one can list Westcott, Plummer, Schlatter, Lagrange, Bernard, Kragerud, and Wilkens."[49]

Therefore, there really seems little logical doubt based on the ever-present inclusion of this chapter in all editions, the existence of an epilogue, and consistent linguistic style that persists throughout the gospel and into chapter 21, that this chapter was authored by anyone other than St. John, like the rest of the gospel. To say otherwise makes little common sense. All of these facts point to his authorship. It seems usual that anyone would suggest otherwise. Perhaps the odd nature of the chapter, how it does not fit with the previous chapter, has caused people to question whether John wrote it. It is a way to search for answers about the unusual events recorded in it. Instead of questioning whether he wrote it, we need to figure out what happened between chapter 20 and chapter 21. If we can bridge the narrative gap between the two chapters it will make the events at the end of the gospel seem more logical and leave little doubt that indeed it was John who was the witness to these miraculous events. The only way to get across that bridge is to examine the chapter itself.

Chapter Three

Rampant Apostasy

"After this"

Expectamus resurrectionem mortuorum et vitam futuri saeculi.[50]

We should mention at the outset that some have put forward the absurd idea that chapter 21 of the Gospel of John is out of order somehow. Some have said that the reason the apostles are giving up in chapter 21 is that story was actually supposed to be put earlier in the gospel and got misplaced at the end. Without having to resort to the argument that divine guidance by the Holy Spirit would make this impossible because the scriptures are handed down as God intended, we can easily disprove this logically.

Chapter 21 is clearly meant to be the end of the gospel. The conclusion of verses 24 and 25 would never fit anywhere except at the end of the gospel. John admits, (as he also did to end the second to last chapter), that there are many more things he could write about that Jesus did. This is the kind of thing you say only at the end. Such a statement would be absurd anywhere else in the text where John is in fact relaying the events of Jesus. It would make no sense to say "there are also many other things that Jesus did, but I do not think the world would contain the books that would be written" and then in fact go on say more things right after you said that. Imagine someone giving a speech and saying "There are so many more things I could say," and then going on to talk for another hour. That type of statement only fits at the end when you are reflecting back at your work, or memories.

Not only that, the Gospel of John is distinctly chronological. Many times John moves the narrative forward in time with a key phrase that he repeats many times, especially at the start of key chapters to tell us that events are moving ahead in time. These two words are "after this." This phrase begins chapters five, six, and seven. Jesus had been in Cana performing another miracle in chapter four. John moves the events both chronically and geographically forward into chapter five by saying "After this, there was a feast of the Jews, and Jesus went up to Jerusalem"[51] (John 5:1). Then as chapter six begins, John moves the action from Jerusalem in chapter five back to Galilee, by saying "After this, Jesus went across the Sea of Galilee (of Tiberius). A large crowd followed him, because they saw the signs he was performing on the sick"[52] (John 6:1-2). The beloved disciple follows this pattern again in chapter seven taking us from Galilee in chapter six back to Jerusalem in chapter seven. "After this, Jesus moved about within Galilee; but he did not wish to travel in Judea, because the Jews were trying to kill him"[53] (John 7:1). Jesus went to Jerusalem anyway, nearly getting himself arrested. This same pattern is repeated as chapter 20 transitions into chapter 21. The evangelist begins chapter 21 by using again that key phrase "after this," telling us that events are moving forward in time just like with chapters five, six, and seven.

Also, the other evidentiary point to make here that proves we are moving forward in time is that the action is transitioning from Jerusalem to Galilee. When there is movement between these two geographical locations like in chapters five, six, and seven, John uses the phrase "after this" to move the reader forward in time as the location changes between these two sacred places. That same geographical movement pattern takes place between chapter 20 and chapter 21, as the action moves from Jerusalem to Galilee yet again. So whenever there is movement by Jesus between Jerusalem and Galilee, like in all of these chapters, John brings us forward in time by using the phrase "after this." This is yet another Johannine parallel that we can make between chapter 21 and other parts of the gospel that lends even more credence to his authorship. By starting chapter 21 by saying "after this" the author is signaling to his readers the fact that some important events are moving forward in time that have built off the previous chapter's proceedings. He is telling us that movement is taking place between Jerusalem and Galilee, or vice versa. In fact, given the pattern from chapters five, six, and seven, it would be unusual if chapter 21 did not begin with "after this."

In the final analysis, those two words were deliberately put there to show us that we are moving forward in time from the events of the previous chapter, like he had done several times before. We even see this same pattern in John 3:11-13 where the action again moves from Galilee to Jerusalem. "Jesus did this as the beginning of his signs in Cana in Galilee and so revealed his glory, and his disciples began to believe in him. After this, he and his mother, brothers, and his disciples went down to Capernaum and stayed there only a few days. Since the Passover was near, Jesus went up to Jerusalem"[54] (John 3:11-13).

If this is not enough evidence, there is a final trump card we can play that proves beyond any doubt that chapter 21 is in its proper order. After John goes through the initial portion of chapter 21 when Jesus appears to his disciples at the Sea of Tiberius, John tells us directly "This was now the third time Jesus was revealed to his disciples after being raised from the dead"[55] (John 21:14). Checkmate. That places this chronologically after his two appearances in the upper room mentioned in the previous chapter. This leaves us no doubt that chapter 21 is in its proper order.

And this is not the only time John tells us that events are moving forward in time chronologically. There is no need to go through the entire gospel to make this point, but a few salient examples might include the following. "The next day he saw Jesus coming toward him and said, 'Behold the Lamb of God, who takes away the sin of the world'"[56] (John 1:29). "The next day he decided to go to Galilee, and he found Philip. And Jesus said to him, 'Follow me'" (John 1:43). "After the two days, he left there for Galilee"[57] (John 4:43). And chapter 18 and 19 are obviously clear examples of the chronological order of how Jesus spent His last days getting arrested, put on trial, and crucified. Simply put, of all the arguments meant to undermine chapter 21, to somehow say that is it out of order, seems the most counterintuitive.

Having established that this final scene with Jesus is in its proper order, we know then that when the apostles reach Galilee, when they go back home, they have already witnessed the previous two appearances of Jesus. We know that they should be starting the work of the church. Instead they chose quite a different path.

"I am going fishing."

Apostasy is defined as the renunciation of a religious faith, the abandonment of a previous loyalty, or defection.[58] In chapter 21 of the Gospel of John the Catholic Church is dead. There is no hope. Nothing but despair, anguish, and treason are in the air. Yet somehow by the end of this miraculous chapter, Jesus has saved His church and brought both Himself and His church back to life.

John is going to twice make it clear that he is deliberately withholding information from his readers. He coyly tells us just before the mysterious chapter 21 begins that "Jesus did many other signs in the presence of (his) disciples that are not written in this book"[59] (John 21:30). Then he says it again at the end of the gospel, noting that "there are many other things that Jesus did, but if these were to be described individually, I do not think the whole world would contain the books that would be written"[60] (John 21:25).

To be clear, the thesis I am putting forward here is that the Catholic Church should have begun at the end of chapter 20 in the Gospel of John. As we just argued and demonstrated above, all the elements are there for the apostles to begin their mission.

But then sometime shortly after this, Jesus gets captured and killed a second time by His own choosing to test the faith of the apostles, and protect them from assassination. The proof of this is that there would be no reason for the apostles to commit utter apostasy in chapter 21 unless they believed Jesus was dead. They would not have given up the cause so readily unless He was taken from them a second time. To make this argument though we must prove beyond any doubt that what is going on chapter 21 is in fact utter apostasy. If it is anything other than that, then this thesis makes little sense. The entire crux of this argument depends largely on seeing how deeply the apostles gave up, in stark contrast to the hope and promise of the previous chapter. Let us then begin this task.

We can start with theologian Sir Edwyn Hoskyns again. "One has betrayed the Lord to death, all except the Beloved Disciple had fled, and now at the suggestion of Simon, the seven who remain together go back to their fishing," Hoskyns writes. "The scene is one of complete apostasy."[61] Fellow theologian, E. A. McDowell, writing in the *Review and Expositor*, one of the longest running religious journals in the United States, offers a similar point of view. He says that the "present tense of the verb 'to go' expresses more than momentary intention." According to McDowell "Peter is going back to his earlier way of life and will stay with it."[62]

In this chapter Simon Peter has made the momentous decision to leave Jerusalem. St. Luke even tells us in the Acts of the Apostles that Christ specifically forbade them to do this. "While meeting with them (the apostles), he enjoined them not to depart from Jerusalem, but to wait for the promise of the Father about which you have heard me speak'"[63] (Acts 1:4). Two dramatic appearances from Jesus apparently were not enough. If Peter and the others were going to begin their life as priests, as holy messengers, Jerusalem is where it would begin. In fact, just read the first two chapters of the Acts of the Apostles for proof of this.

Galilee would not be the place to begin recruiting. In fact, after this final appearance the apostles left the Sea of Tiberius to return to Jerusalem to begin preaching the good news of Jesus. In other words, they are not going back home for missionary work. In fact no such mention of that is talked about in chapter 21. They are going back home to return to their former lives. Again, it is like Washington's men deserting him before the battle of Trenton. Like Washington, Jesus needed a similar miracle to rally his troops who were also going back home. Simon says, "I am going fishing" (John 21:3). Those are probably the most heart-breaking words in the Bible. This means that he is giving up. That he has had enough. His savior has been killed a second time and he just cannot take it anymore. It is time to go back home, and to try to recapture his former way of life as a fisherman. This is all that is left, all that he can think to do at this point. In fact, if the apostles were not giving up, there would be no need for Jesus to appear to them again here.

It is also quite disturbing that Simon leaves with the entire corps group including Nathanael, James, John, and two other disciples who John spares the shame of naming. Importantly, the final key part of this rogue group is Thomas, also known as Didymus. John has just got though telling us about the recently acquired unbending faith of this man, of how Jesus made a specific example out of him, and had convinced even him. The fact that Thomas is in this group is not a good sign. If he is giving up too, then something is seriously wrong with this scene. Nothing short of death could cause such a convert to so readily follow the herd. "We also will come with you," (John 21:3) all these men sheepishly reply when Peter tells them that he is going fishing. Notice that Peter says, "I am going fishing," not "we are all going fishing so follow me." This implies that the group has already split up. Peter is going back home with or without them. He does not even seem to have an interest in keeping the 11 together as a unit. Four other men are missing, and unaccounted for. He is not ordering them to follow him back home to Galilee. It is almost as if he really could not care any less if they came with him. Keep in mind this is the appointed, hand-picked "rock" that the Church will be built on, and at this moment his leadership is severely lacking. Perhaps there might even be some anger on the part of Peter, some disillusionment with Jesus that he had tried his best, but it was simply time to give up. And we need to keep in mind that the course he is choosing, the path he is taking is one of complete and utter disrespect to Jesus. He and the others are making a conscious decision here to sin against Jesus. What else but utter despair could cause them to make this choice? They are going back to the beginning of it all, where three short years ago this mystical man had called them away from their lives as fishermen. He specifically told them that this life was not for them any longer, that they were not to go back to it. All of His preaching and His resurrection would mean nothing if they would simply retire back to their lives as fishermen and not tell the world what they saw and heard about their savior. From now on they would be fishers of men. "Do not be afraid, from now on you will be catching men. When they brought their boats to the shore they left everything and followed him" (Luke 5:10-11). Jesus does not say, "from now until you decide to give up or change your minds." This was a life they could not go back to. Jesus says in Luke chapter 9 to another potential follower, "And another said, 'I will follow you Lord, but first let me say farewell to my family at home. Jesus said, 'No one who sets a hand to the plow and looks to what was left behind is fit for the kingdom of God" (Luke 9:61-62).

So the proof that the apostles were committing apostasy falls into three different realms. The first is that they chose to leave Jerusalem to return to their former lives, which Jesus had explicitly forbidden them to do, as was just explained above. The second way to prove that the Catholic Church was dead, that the eleven believed that Jesus had died a second time is that the apostles fractured apart in chapter 21. If Christ had simply left them and ascended to Heaven, they would begin together the enormous task of preaching that commences in the Acts of the Apostles. Something much more drastic must have happened to Jesus to cause this group to not only give up, go back home, but also to splinter apart. They must have believed that He was dead to take such a radical course of action. Perhaps after Thomas saw how real He was, that also meant that to them His flesh and blood could be killed again. John reports that not all of the apostles followed Peter, the appointed leader, back to Galilee. Only seven did. The other four chose not to. John probably reported the news that Christ had been captured again and this may have tipped off a heated argument among the eleven about what to do next. They had already lost Him once. Peter had recently denied Jesus three times and seems to waste little time heading back to his former life. As we will see later, Jesus at several different points in chapter 21 is extremely angry at Peter for choosing this course of action, asking at one point if he even loves Him anymore. This dramatic fracturing is essential to our understanding of the situation at hand. Four of the apostles deliberately chose not to stay with the other seven men. There is nothing left to hold them together. If this was a missionary trip or a just a trip to get food they would all go together, and such a mundane excursion would never even need to be put as the culmination of the entire gospel. Moreover, as we will examine below, the very need for Jesus to appear to them, plus His words and subsequent actions prove that they were giving up.

The third way to prove that the apostles were giving up then is to examine how the fracturing of these men took place. If the remaining eleven apostles were ever going to permanently split apart and return back to their former lives, they would logically break apart into a seven – three – one – split. That is exactly what John reports happening in chapter 21. Seven apostles return to Galilee, while four others are missing and unaccounted for. It is likely that John did not even know where the other four had gone at that point. Let us therefore examine why if the apostles were going to permanently break apart, it would be along the lines reported in chapter 21. To do this, we need to briefly examine their lives.

John reports that he, his brother James, Peter, Nathanael, Thomas, and two other apostles, who he mysteriously does not name, all return back to their former lives as fishermen. All of these men lived and grew up in Galilee, mostly in and around Bethsaida. It is not all that difficult to figure out who the other two men were who John does not name. Logic dictates that they must have been Andrew and Philip. Andrew was Peter's brother, and also a fisherman from Bethsaida. In fact, he of course introduced Peter to Jesus. Philip makes sense as the other candidate because he too was a fisherman from Bethsaida, like the others.[64] These seven men knew each other long before they even met Jesus and probably all went to school together as children.

That leaves us with James the younger, Jude, Simon, and Matthew. Let us deal with Matthew first. He of course was not a fisherman, but instead a Roman tax collector who would have little interest in following Peter back to Galilee to start a new life as a fisherman. It is also likely that James the younger, Jude, and Matthew would stay together because they probably were all brothers.[65] Also James, Jude, and Simon all had radical tendencies that were unique only to them among the remaining eleven men. Jude and Simon were Zealots. Jude was a violent nationalist with the dream of domination and world power by the Jewish people. In John 14:22, he asked Jesus at the Last Supper, "But Lord, why do you intend to show yourself to us and not to the world?" Jude was interested in making Christ known to the world, not as a suffering messiah, but as a ruling military leader.[66] Simon had a similar world view, making him an easy attachment to this group. In fact, he was known as Simon the Zealot.

The Zealots were fanatical Jewish Nationalists who had heroic disregard for the suffering involved and the struggle for what they regarded as the purity of their faith. The Zealots were crazed with hatred for the Romans. It was this hate for Rome that destroyed the city of Jerusalem. Josephus says the Zealots were reckless persons, zealous in good practices and extravagant and reckless in the worst kind of actions. From this background, we see that Simon was a fanatical Nationalist, a man devoted to the Law, a man with bitter hatred for anyone who dared to compromise with Rome.[67]

As for James the younger he was also known to have a fiery personality which is perhaps what got him martyred in Egypt. His apostolic symbol is the saw since tradition holds that his body was sawed into pieces.[68] Therefore James, Jude, Simon, and Matthew seem to fit together nicely. Three of them were likely brothers and the forth, Simon, fits in with the radical points of view of at least one of these brothers, or perhaps two. Little is known about James the younger. If his brother Jude was a Zealot is it likely that was at least exposed to these ideas as well. Matthew may have gone off on his own, not having any Zealot tendencies, or perhaps chose to stay at least temporarily with his brothers. Either way, these four form a logical group. Three are related to each other, and the third shares the political philosophy of at least one other member of this group of four. In the final analysis, if the apostles were going to break up, these four men would likely band together and go off on their own given their kinship, and their background in Zealotry which did not exist within the seven fishermen who headed to Galilee. Therefore the fact the John reports that seven men head to Galilee is extremely significant. It points to a profound breakup along political and kinship lines that appear to be tearing the apostles apart without the leadership of Jesus, and I dare say Judas as well.

It is also interesting that John does not name Andrew and Philip as the other men who accompany Peter to Galilee. It is possible that he wants to spare them the shame of naming them among the seven traitors. Certainly this is a deliberate choice to fail to give their names. I suspect that if he tells us that it was in fact Andrew and Philip, then we would get an even better sense of how desperate this situation really was. It would confirm the logical and devastating split among the apostles along kinship and political lines that I suspect John wanted to cover up. It was bad enough that four had defected, and deliberately chose not to follow Peter. It was bad enough that the group had fractured without confirming how deep and profound the chasm was. Leaving two names ambiguous could give the illusion that there was still some hope that the eleven would at one point form a single unit again.

When the seven return to Galilee they immediately begin fishing, but catch nothing. Try as they might to begin their old lives again, it is impossible without Christ. Jesus has made it so they cannot resume their former profession. Only when He appears to them do they catch any fish. It is only through Him that they can continue in any fashion. The attempt to go back to their former lives completely fails because it is devoid of Jesus. If they were simply going back to get food or begin missionary work they would have caught fish without needing Christ to be there. The initial inability to catch fish is proof that Jesus is gone from their lives, absent from their intentions. They are simply fisherman at that point, and failing even at that, a profession they had mastered years ago. It was only when Christ made His third and final appearance to them here that they once again became fishers of men and abandoned this attempt to return back to where it was safe and comfortable.

Further proof that they are no longer "fishers of men" is how Jesus first addresses them in a markedly condescending way. They are no longer men to Him, but children because that is how they are behaving. "Children, have you caught anything to eat?"[69] (John 21:4). One has to wonder how long Jesus was standing there. Was He there all night, watching their futile efforts to go on without Him? Was He watching in horror, or somehow amused at their increasing frustration as these professional fisherman caught nothing hour after hour?

It is revealing that when Jesus appears to them here it seems as if John already knows what is going to happen. He is like a co-conspirator and one has to wonder if John was standing there on the shore with Jesus, accounting for how he could report so clearly what Christ was saying to the apostles. How could John hear all this dialogue from Christ if he was in one of the boats with the other men? Did John know that Jesus would be appearing that morning and was waiting for his master to show up? Was his faith that strong? John was the first to say to Peter, "It is the Lord"[70] (John 21:7). It is impossible to know how he said this, but I imagine at that moment John realized that everything was going to be alright now. That whatever plan he may have taken part in to allow his master to suffer again had worked out just fine. Peter's reaction was to wildly jump into the water to rush towards his master. This reaction indicates that Peter must have thought Christ was dead. What other conclusion makes more logical sense? There was no such outward display of emotions in either of the previous two appearances that John recorded. This third appearance seems entirely different. It is filled with unrequited joy on the part of Peter. He is running towards Him through the water, like towards the empty tomb. Running is a sign in the gospels that a miracle has just taken place. If the apostles thought that Jesus was dead that also would account for the fact that they initially did not recognize Him standing on the shore, or recognize His voice. "When it was already dawn, Jesus was standing on the shore; but the disciples did not realize that is was Jesus"[71] (John 21:4). He would be the last person they would expect if they thought He was dead.

Furthermore, they are filled with shame for doubting that He would return again. This is another indication that they thought He was dead. "And none of the disciples dared to ask him, 'Who are you?' because they realized it was the Lord."[72] There is no such shame recorded in either of the two previous appearances. The apostles seem almost afraid of Him as they have breakfast, in awe of the fact that He was miraculously returned to them again. They are ashamed that they have given up on Him again. Their shame further proves their apostasy. Now for a third time though, Christ has not given up on them. Yet there is still work to be done in these final moments with His friends.

What follows are a series of actions that demonstrate that Jesus is going to use this final appearance to rebuild His church and start it anew right there on the shores of the Sea of Tiberius. This will be a fresh start for everyone as He will commission these men again to safely start preaching the good news. Symbolically everything is set for a new beginning. Instead of breaking bread and sharing wine at the Last Supper, Jesus shares a breakfast of fish at dawn with these men. This is a sign of their new beginning. Instead of preparing them for His death, like at the Last Supper, he is preparing them for their new life as priests, commissioning them to start preaching the gospel. Christ shares with them a breakfast from the 153 fish the apostles caught. Greek zoologists at the time catalogued 153 different species of fish known to humankind.[73] These fish symbolized all the different nations and types of people that the apostles will now preach to. They will once again be "fishers of men."

It is interesting that the Catholic Church accords so much relevance and respect to the Last Supper. The meal of bread and wine that literally are transfixed into the Body and Blood of Christ at every Catholic mass hearken back to those final hours before Christ was crucified. The mass is in many ways a re-creation of the Last Supper, an event that set the stage for His death, crucifixion, and resurrection. It was a somber scene filled with ominous overtones as Jesus prepared Himself for the suffering He surely knew was just hours away. This breakfast of fish shared with most of these same men is meant to be the polar opposite of the Last Supper. Instead of blood and death we have new life. Jesus shares a breakfast at dawn instead of a supper at dusk. The Last Supper was inside in an upper room, whereas this breakfast is shared outside in the open air on the ground. The Last Supper was planned and prepared ahead of time likely by women loyal to Jesus, whereas this breakfast was prepared spontaneously by the apostles and Jesus themselves. The Last Supper was a lengthy meal filled with a lot of conversation and time spent celebrating the ritual of the Passover, whereas this breakfast was simpler in its rituals. These men ate fish, a symbol of new life, instead of wine into blood, and bread becoming Christ's suffering body. The symbol of the fish here is the key to our understanding of the event here. They will eat fish here because at this meal they will become fishers of men again. This breakfast is a new start for everyone. Jesus had already showed them that he could miraculously feed a throng of people with just a few fish, so this meal would have special meaning because of that as well. The Greek word for fish (ICHTUS), works as an acrostic. An acrostic is a composition in which certain letters in each line form a word or words.[74] **I** = Jesus, **C** = Christ, **TH** = God's, **U** = Son, **S** = Savior.[75] In other words Jesus uses the food at each meal to symbolize Himself, but in very different ways. The bread and wine at the Last Supper were His very body and blood to shed for all of mankind within hours of the meal. The fish at the breakfast was also a symbol of Himself, but instead of death, the fish symbolized new life. Christians and fish are born in water, plus Jesus is able to literally manifest fish into life, to create them where they did not exist before. He gives these fish here life itself to share a meal with His friends. The apostles eat the fish and bread that Jesus brought with Him, and prepared for them. The bread and fish literally come from Him and therefore are symbols of Him. This meal was meant to celebrate His second resurrection with most of the same men who were at the Last Supper.

Another opposite aspect to this is that the breakfast is after the second resurrection, whereas the Last Supper was before the first resurrection. Christ uses both of these meals to set the stage for what He has planned for these men to do next. At the Last Supper he instructs Judas to begin the process for His being handed over, and tells the apostles what is going to happen in the coming hours. At the "First Breakfast," if you will, Christ will use this time to get Peter back to the rock that He can build the Church on. This breakfast will make them once again fishers of men. We should not underestimate the importance of this meal. Before it they were done with Him. After it, they are once again His apostles and ready to preach the good news again. Is it too much to propose that this meal has at least equal importance then as the Last Supper does? Should we as Catholics be reenacting not just the Last Supper every Sunday, but perhaps once a year reenact this breakfast as well? I also suspect that the early Christians knew of the importance of this event. Perhaps that is why the fish was a secret Catholic symbol put outside the homes of many early Christians. The fish is one of the earliest and most sacred of all Catholic symbols. Many a Catholic would draw half an arc in the sand, and the other person would complete the arc, making it a fish, and they knew they were safe. The fish was a less obvious symbol than the cross, allowing some to avoid persecution by the Romans.[76] Yet could this breakfast be another reason for the use of this fish? Did early Catholics understand the importance of this meal and sought to remember it through this symbol?

I would like to propose a more distinguished name for this most sacred event. Instead of First Breakfast, we will go with the Latin translation of "Primus Prandium"[77] in all future references in this text. Like at the Last Supper, Primus Prandium also features Jesus and the apostles eating bread. This is meant by John to symbolically tie these two events together. Jesus breaks and shares bread with His apostles at both meals. The bread is meant to symbolize His suffering body for both the first and second deaths. This event tells us not only that He has suffered twice, but also the manner in which He likely suffered. Notice that there is nothing to drink at this meal, unlike at the Last Supper. The bread and wine at the Last Supper showed us that Jesus' body was attacked, and His blood was shed. This foreshadowed the manner in which He died. In a similar way, can we then assume that Primus Prandium would also give the manner in which Jesus died a second time? Was the manner of death in which Jesus died a second time devoid of blood since there was nothing to drink at this breakfast? Was He, like the fish He shared with these men, born again in water? Having been baptized by John, did He choose to rise again after having been drowned by the Romans, or the Jews? The symbolic power of such a death would likely appeal to Jesus as well as the Romans who would probably not choose crucifixion a second time, having seen how it obviously failed the first time. The Last Supper gives us bread and wine for His body and blood. Primus Prandium gives us bread and fish for His body given new life, risen again in water.

Yet another powerful opposite aspect between the supper and the breakfast is what happens next with Peter. After the Last Supper concluded, John records how Peter denies Jesus three times in the hours that immediately follow the conclusion of the Last Supper. This is in chapter 18 of the Gospel of John. In an opposite manner, this time not after supper but after breakfast, Peter makes a threefold confession to Jesus that he loves Jesus and will do anything for Him to counteract his three denials from earlier. John records this dramatic confrontation between Jesus and his handpicked successor, the man who will have to see to it that the Catholic Church is going to survive long after Jesus is gone. The anger that Christ displays here toward Peter is further evidence that the apostles had given up. Jesus obviously knew that they were all sitting there on the shores of Tiberius because of Peter. "The rock" had been the one to give up, and the one to deny Him three times. The foundation of the church was the one who led six other men back to their former lives, in a complete betrayal of what the master had specifically forbidden them to do. Three times in this passage Christ directly asks Peter if he loves Him, and three times Peter insists that he still does. The master tells Peter, "feed my lambs"[78] (John 21:15), "tend my sheep"[79] (John 21:16), and "feed my sheep"[80] (John 21:17). In fact, when Jesus first says to Peter, "Simon, son of John, do you love me more than these?"[81] (John 21:15), He was asking Peter if he loves fishing more than Him. In other words, "do you love all these things more than me?" Perhaps Jesus even gestured to the boats and the nets around them while saying this. Jesus was instructing Peter to take good care of His church, and all of its followers since Peter will now be the head of it once Christ is gone. The fact that Jesus feels the need to do this is further evidence that the church was all but dead before He made this third appearance to the apostles. In fact, the First Vatican Council said that these verses gave Peter jurisdiction as supreme shepherd of the flock, in other words pope.[82] This implies that such power was lacking before this conversation; that Peter had given up his previously assigned role as leader by returning to fishing. Jesus once again makes him the ruler over the flock. This is further proof that they had committed apostasy. Such a pep talk is unnecessary given the previous two appearances and the gift of the Holy Spirit given to the apostles in His first appearance. Instead Jesus knew how desperate this situation was and felt the need to make sure Peter was prepared for the work ahead. Jesus also makes it clear that Peter is going to die an old man as a messenger of God, not a fisherman. "He said this signifying what kind of death he would glorify God. And when he had said this, he said to him, 'Follow me'"[83] (John 21:19). Follow Christ, and not this former life you had gone back to.

42

John follows this up with the final recorded scene in his gospel. This is yet another angry confrontation between Jesus and Peter. There is clearly a lot of tension between these two men conveyed in this testy exchange. John was following Jesus after the meal had broken up, and Peter strangely asks Jesus regarding John, "What about him?"[84] (John 21:21). Perhaps Peter wondered who was going to take care of this young man, or why Jesus had not been so angry with John. Jesus sharply answered, "What concern is it of yours? You follow me"[85] (John 21:22).

Unlike Mark's and Luke's gospel there is no mention of the Ascension in John's narrative. I suspect this is a deliberate choice. Without the Ascension it gives the chapter's ending a sense of deliberate continued forward momentum into a renewed future where the apostles will continue to follow Jesus. There is a lack of closure here, a sense that Jesus wants to remain a little while longer to make sure they will not be back on his instructions to "follow me." John does not tell us what happens next, but by the time they get back to Jerusalem, their master has left them for good with a promise to return. Perhaps He would have a fourth time if they needed Him to, but their faith prevailed through the work Jesus did to rebuild His church in this final appearance.

If they had not given up, if they had not fractured, there would be no need for Christ to appear to them here, like He did twice before when He appeared to the apostles after the crucifixion. It is also truly awe-inspiring the level of patience and faith Jesus had in these men who misunderstood Him, had fallen asleep on Him during his time of need, denied Him, and blatantly given up on Him. He does not quit on them. In fact, I suspect He may have even made an appearance to the other four men who were missing from this scene. Is the lost ending to the Gospel of Mark really an appearance to Simon, Jude, and James the younger, and perhaps Matthew? We can never truly know, but it is important to speculate how the word got back to the other four that Jesus had returned again. In fact, St. Luke reports in Acts chapter one that all the apostles have returned to Jerusalem and reformed for the purpose of preaching and picking a successor to Judas Iscariot. It is interesting that when naming the apostles and describing how they had returned to the upper room where they were staying he lists Peter, John, James, Andrew, Philip, Thomas, and Nathanael first. This was the group that went to Galilee. Then he completes the list by naming Matthew, James the younger, Simon, and Jude in that order. That cannot be a coincidence. Does this confirm the analysis from earlier? It certainly adds some credence to it. The list is another seven to four split. Luke sees the breakdown with the apostles in the same way. Perhaps he was reporting the order in which these men arrived, or that the other four showed up sometime after the seven fishermen came back from Galilee. This is in Acts 1:13.[86]

Therefore we have logically concluded that the apostles had given up, gone back to their previous lives, and fractured apart into two predictable sects in a show of complete and utter apostasy. There would be no reason for this unless they assumed Jesus was dead, given the fact that He had appeared to them two previous times in the time prior to this third and final appearance by Him. Christ had given them all that they needed to begin spreading the news of His resurrection to start the process of building the Catholic Church. And yet in the very next scene in the gospel of John that very same church is dead, fractured, and missing in action. The fact that Christ appeared a third time to these men proves they had given up. Only His death could have caused such a complete betrayal of his specific instructions not to leave Jerusalem and not to return to their former lives as fishermen. Only His death could have given them the confidence to take such a drastic step as apostasy.

The reverse order theory

When would this second resurrection take place? Obviously it would have to be between the second and third appearance in the

Gospel of John, in other words sometime between chapters 20 and 21. John tells us that the first appearance to the apostles was on the evening of Easter Sunday. "On the evening of that first day of the week, when the doors were locked, where the disciples were, for fear of the Jews, Jesus came and stood in their midst and said to them, 'Peace be with you'"[87] (John 20:19). The second appearance was a week after this. "Now a week later his disciples were again inside and Thomas was with them"[88] (John 20:26). Therefore, at that point seven days had passed since Jesus rose from the dead. Luke tells us in Acts 1:3[89] that Jesus spent forty days on earth before the Ascension. That leaves 33 days from the second appearance in John's gospel until the time of the Ascension. We do not know when the third appearance took place. All that we can logically conclude is that it was after the second appearance. Can we assume that having completed His work after the third appearance, Christ would not need any more time with the apostles? The mission was complete. His work was finally over. Logically there would be no need to spend any more time on earth. It is likely that the evening of the third appearance would be a logical time for the Ascension. This makes much better sense than what the Gospel of Mark and the Gospel of Luke say. Both of these authors claim that the Ascension took place on Easter Sunday night. That could not possibly be true given what John tells us about the appearances of Christ which took place over the course of many weeks. Luke in the Acts of the apostles even says that Christ stayed on earth for forty days. I also do not believe it is possible to know exactly where the Ascension took place only that it makes sense to place it immediately after the third appearance given the fact that Jesus' work was done. Also by placing the Gospel of John just before the Acts of Apostles, the Catholic Church implies through the continued narrative here that the third appearance was Jesus' last action on this earth before the Ascension. Notice that the Gospel of Luke is not placed before the Acts of the Apostles which would have made better narrative sense given the fact that they were meant to flow together as a single text by one author, namely St. Luke. Instead, the third appearance is the last moment before the Ascension is recorded in the Acts of Apostles. The implication then is that these events follow into each other chronologically. If Luke and Acts were placed back to back it would draw attention to the discrepancies between his two versions of the Ascension.

I do not see any problem with Primus Prandium and the Ascension both transpiring on the fortieth day, no matter where it took place. Jesus was at the Sea of Tiberius that morning with His apostles completing His final work on this earth. If there was another appearance, John would have told us about it. The Ascension here in front of His apostles in their hometown makes a lot of sense. This was where the mission began, and this was where it would end. This was exactly where He recruited them. "As he passed by the Sea of Galilee (Sea of Tiberius), he saw Simon and his brother Andrew casting their nets into the sea; they were fishermen. Jesus said to them, "Come after me, and I will make you fishers of men'"[90] (Mark 1:16-17). It makes sense that Christ would want to leave them here, at this most sacred of locations to end His time on this earth at the place He made them fishers of men. This of course would contradict the gospel accounts. Mark absurdly has Jesus ascending to heaven on Easter Sunday, but never says exactly where it would have been, so that does not really help answer the question of location. We should note however that most historians agree that the true ending to the Gospel of Mark has been lost to history so we will never really know if the author had anything to say about where the Ascension took place. The Gospel of Luke says that the Ascension took place on Easter Sunday night when Jesus led the apostles "out as far as Bethany, raised his hands and blessed them"[91] (Luke 24:50). If we can agree that this simply could have taken place on Easter Sunday night then how can we trust Luke to get the location correct, if he has the date wrong? Then he gives a completely different account of the Ascension in the Acts of Apostles which I think further undermines his credibility. In this account the Ascension is on day forty, and is no longer in Bethany but instead on the Mount of Olives which is a mile and half from the village of Bethany.[92] Also this account includes more dialogue from Jesus, and the appearance of two angels that Luke somehow forgot to mention in his first account. Another purpose for the church to put the Gospel of John between Luke and Acts is to distract attention from these obvious discrepancies. If the two books were placed together, the two accounts of the Ascension would be read one after the other. Luke gives us different times, locations, and participants in both accounts written within paragraphs of each other. How can any logically thinking person not question this? To be clear, I am not saying that the Ascension never happened. Jesus clearly intended that to be His final act on this earth as John tells us in 20:17. All I am proposing is that the location of this key event may not be where Luke says it took place. If he is wrong about timing in his gospel, how we trust the location? And if he is so contradictory of his own previous account, how can we give credibility to it? Luke also was not a witness to these events, never having been one of Jesus' apostles. Did John mention that the Ascension took place along the shores of the Sea of Tiberius, but church leaders took this passage out, so as not to contradict what Luke hacked his way through with his own contradictory accounts? Also consider that Matthew has no account of the Ascension in his gospel. That seems quite strange, and quite telling. Remember that he was not with the apostles for this third appearance. He stayed behind, likely in Jerusalem with Jude, Simon, and James. If the Ascension took place along the shores of the Sea of Tiberius he would have no direct knowledge of it, never having been there. This would account for him not mentioning the Ascension in his gospel.

Even if we want to take Luke at his word and agree that the ascension took place on the Mount of Olives, I still think we can conclude that it is entirely possible that Primus Prandium and the Ascension could both still take place on the fortieth day. This takes a little more work, but we can still get this one to the garage too. The distance between Bethsaida and the Mount of Olives is 155 km.[93] John tells us that Jesus had the ability to appear inside locked rooms. His resurrected body made appearances regardless of time and space. I do not see any problem with Jesus being able to appear on the shores of Galilee that morning, and then on the Mount of Olives that night, if the Son of God chose to do so. His supernatural abilities are without question. To say that this would be beyond His capability would be counterintuitive. Luke is also vague about who exactly was at the Ascension. Not having witnessed it himself, he does not name the apostles who were there in either of his accounts. He probably did not know who exactly was there, only telling us that one of the angels says "men of Galilee"[94] (Acts 1:11). Is it possible that these "men of Galilee" were none other than Jude, Simon the Zealot, James the younger, and perhaps Matthew as well? All of these apostles were from Galilee.[95] These were the men who did not go back to Galilee, and instead stayed behind in Jerusalem. Were these three or four men the ones who witnessed the Ascension? Is this why John says nothing about the Ascension simply because he, like the other six men, was not there when it happened? These three men (not so much Matthew) would probably need the most convincing to spread the word of Christ. A dramatic display of Jesus' love and power in His final moments on earth reserved for these elect, would be all that it would take. Also consider the possibility that these apostles did not give up, that they may have stayed in Jerusalem to continue the cause. Perhaps Jesus felt that they were the only ones who deserved to witness the Ascension, much like He chose favorites for His transfiguration. After His first resurrection Jesus made sure to visit the apostles twice because Thomas was missing during the first visit. This same scenario is what might be happening here after the second resurrection, namely two visits, Primus Prandium and the Ascension. It is likely that Jesus would want to visit with these four men who were missing from the breakfast before he left to be with His Father. Either way, whether the Ascension took place in Galilee or Bethany, we can logically conclude that Primus Prandium and the Ascension most likely took place on the same day, the fortieth day since Jesus' resurrection.

Therefore we can conclude that 33 days transpired between the second appearance on day seven, and the third appearance at the Sea of Galilee on day forty. The number 33 also makes sense symbolically given the traditional assumption that Jesus lived 33 years and 3 is the number of the Holy Trinity. In other words a little over a month went by during that time. There is no possible way that we can logically conclude that Christ would chose to spend that large amount of time on this earth unless He felt there was important work to be done.

We have also just gone through demonstrating how John intended Primus Prandium to be the polar opposite of the Last Supper. This was a celebration of Jesus returning from the dead a second time, instead of a preparation for His first death like the Last Supper. Notice that there was no such symbolically laden meal recorded in either of the first two appearances Jesus had with His apostles. It was only this third one that had this meal. If Jesus wanted to celebrate His return from death with a meal He could have done so in either of those appearances. John is telling us that the third time was radically different, featuring a meal just as important as the Last Supper. Another striking feature about Primus Prandium is when it occurred. As demonstrated above, I feel confident in saying that the Ascension took place on the evening of the third appearance, making that Jesus' fortieth day on this earth after His resurrection. If you count day one as a Sunday when He rose from the dead, and then keep counting the days until you get to forty, which of course we are saying here is the day of the Ascension and Primus Prandium, we land on a Thursday. That gives us our final striking polar opposite of these two meals. That would mean that the Last Supper took place on a Thursday night and Primus Prandium took place on a Thursday morning. That cannot be a coincidence. Both were on a Thursday at opposite ends of the day.

Let us review then how many aspects of the Last Supper and Primus Prandium are at polar opposites of each other. John is telling us that these meals are of equal importance which we have demonstrated above when we explained how Christ re-commissioned the apostles at this breakfast, especially Peter. The apostles eat a breakfast instead of a supper. They eat at dawn instead of dusk. They eat outside on the ground instead of inside in an upper room. They have bread and fish to eat instead of bread and wine. The breakfast is short with little dialogue instead of the long discourse of the Last Supper. Jesus prepares the meal instead of the meal being prepared for them at the Last Supper. The Last Supper prepared for Jesus' death, while Primus Prandium celebrated their new life together. The Last Supper was before the first resurrection while Primus Prandium was after the second resurrection. After the Last Supper Peter denies Jesus three times, while after Primus Prandium Peter affirms his love for Jesus three times. There was wine to drink at the Last Supper, while there was nothing to drink at the breakfast. The Last Supper occurred on Thursday night, while Primus Prandium occurred on a Thursday morning.

If everything then is opposite here, even the timing, we can extrapolate even further. John is giving us a secret code here for when Jesus died a second time. Logically then the timing of when Jesus would be killed and resurrected a second time would play out backwards in time as well from Primus Prandium. If we can take the timetable of the Last Supper, the crucifixion, and the resurrection, then we can mirror this to His second death and resurrection, backwards in time from that sacred breakfast. Because John is saying to us that these two meals are equal in importance, and opposite in timing, then logically the timing must be opposite as well for the first death and second death, as well as the first resurrection and second resurrections. This would give us another Holy Week, a second week of Jesus breaking bread with His apostles, being killed, and resurrected. The main events of the first Holy Week begin with a meal on the night of Holy Thursday, and end with the resurrection on Easter Sunday morning. So we start with a meal on a Thursday night and end with life on a Sunday. If everything is the opposite for the second Holy Week, then we would start with death on a Sunday and end with a meal on a Thursday. In other words, a Sunday would be the day of Jesus' second death, and the second Holy Week would end with a meal on a Thursday morning instead of a Thursday night. That is how this would have to play out if this opposite timing hypothesis is correct. Does it? Yes it does. If we take the timetable of the Last Supper, the crucifixion, and the resurrection and pace it out in reverse order, the timing for a second Holy Week ends up being exactly as the hypothesis laid out above predicts it would be.

Unfortunately, we now have to do a lot of math. Let us start with the Last Supper. The traditional start time for the Passover meal that Jesus was celebrating that night with His apostles is 6 p.m.[96] The crucifixion began at noon on Good Friday and ended at 3 p.m. Jesus rose from the dead on Easter Sunday morning. The exact time is not known, but we will go with 6 a.m. as a logical timeframe which would be around dawn. That means 60 hours transpired between the beginning of the Last Supper and the time of the resurrection. 18 hours elapsed from the time of the Last Supper to the beginning of the crucifixion. 21 hours is the timeframe from the beginning of the Last Supper to the moment of Jesus' death. 42 hours is the time between the beginning of the crucifixion and the moment of the resurrection, while 39 hours would be the timetable between the time of death and moment of new life on Easter Sunday morning.

With that figured out, let us then play out these numbers in reverse order. If the reverse order theory is right, then these numbers should bring us to Sunday as the moment of Jesus' second death, making that a day of death, instead of a day of new life. We will begin with 6 a.m. as dawn is breaking on the fortieth day as that sacred breakfast begins. It is Thursday morning, the end of the second Holy Week. We just calculated that 60 hours transpired between the Last Supper and the resurrection. When then is 60 hours before Primus Prandium? That would give the exact time of Jesus' second resurrection. That brings us to Monday at 6 p.m. of the 37th day after Jesus rose from the dead the first time. If we then take this time backwards we will have the moment of His second death. We will need to go back 39 hours from that point because we calculated that 39 hours transpired from the moment of Jesus' first death to His first resurrection. When then is 39 hours before 6 p.m. on Monday of the 37th day? This would give us the exact moment of Jesus' second death. 39 hours before 6 p.m. on a Monday night brings us to 1 a.m. on Sunday morning of the 36th day. That would be the time of Jesus' second death. This is as we predicted. This proves that the theory is correct. The second Holy Week begins with death on a Sunday, and ends with a meal on a Thursday. The main events of the first Holy Week as we said begin with a meal on a Thursday and end with new life on a Sunday. We should note that everything is symbolically impressive here as well. Logically it would make sense for Christ to pick a Sunday for this to happen. The resurrection, the first appearance, and the second appearance to the apostles all happened on Sundays. This seems to be the day He has chosen to do His Father's work. And if this second death was just meant for the privacy of either Pilate or the Sanhedrin to see, the secrecy of a 1 a.m. death would appeal to all parties involved. This was a private matter for this inner circle to deal with. The 36th day is symbolically important too, given its obvious numerical allusions to the Holy Trinity.

We therefore can logically conclude that the Second Holy Week played out like this, according to what I am going to call The Gospel of John Reverse Order Theory. Day 36, 1 a.m.: time of Jesus' second death. Day 37, 6 p.m.: time of Jesus' second resurrection. Day 40: 6 a.m. Primus Prandium, followed by the evening Ascension, either at the Mount of Olives, or at the Sea of Tiberius. Does it not make logical sense that Christ would reserve the final days on this earth for His most important work? Is it also possible that John was the only one who knew about these events, besides of course Pilate? Maybe the other 10 men did not want to know what happened to their master, or could not comprehend how, or why this had happened. All they had to know was that Jesus was back again. There is so much that we just do not know because John seems to be so reluctant to share all that was shown to him during his short time with Jesus.

The flight from Jerusalem

If Jesus was indeed put to death on the 36th day, another way we could prove that He was killed on that day, would be to somehow find evidence that the 36th day was also the day that the apostles left Jerusalem to return to Bethsaida in Galilee. If we could prove that the 36th day was when something so horrible happened that it caused the apostles to give up, and then fracture apart into two separate groups, then this would lend even more evidence to a second death on that day. If the apostles found out on the 36th day that Christ had been killed again, they would leave within hours of discovering this, after making some basic preparation for their journey back home. The renewed devastation and fear would be so great that it would cause them to leave Jerusalem and fracture apart. We do know that the apostles left Jerusalem for Galilee, that they gave up and fractured apart, but if we place these dramatic events on the day I am saying Jesus died a second time, then it reinforces the potential for day 36 to be the pivotal day. Can we therefore place their departure from Jerusalem on the 36th day?

Let us start with what we know. We have concluded logically that Primus Prandium and the Ascension took place on day 40. According to the Gospel of John, the seven fishermen arrived in Galilee the day before, on Wednesday of the 39th day. They probably came into town sometime in the afternoon or evening because they immediately began fishing that night. Bible scholar Merilyn Hargis writing for *Christian History and Biography* tells us that the journey between Jerusalem and Galilee in the time of Christ was always a three day affair.

Jesus' journeys between Galilee and Jerusalem have been the most misunderstood travel accounts in the Bible. Josephus' reference to a Samaritan attack on a group of Galilean pilgrims going to Jerusalem has often been taken to explain that Jesus' route through Samaria was unusual and risky. Many have asserted that Jews refused to travel through Samaria at all, crossing the Jordan to the east in order to avoid the area they regarded as "unclean." This notion is a myth. The Samaritan attack Josephus referred to happened in A.D. 52, and no such attack had occurred before or during Jesus' lifetime. Even Josephus says, "It was the custom of the Galileans, when they came to the Holy City at the festivals, to take their journeys through the country of the Samaritans." The route from Galilee to Jerusalem via Samaria remained the shortest and easiest route, a journey that took only three days.[97]

Three days before the evening of the 39th day would obviously place us on the evening of the 36th day. The first day of travel would be Sunday into Monday. The second day of travel would be Monday into Tuesday while the third day of travel would be Tuesday into Wednesday. Without question if the apostles arrived in Galilee on the afternoon or evening of Wednesday of the 39th day that means for some reason they chose to leave Jerusalem on the afternoon or evening of the 36th day, the same day we calculated as being the day Christ died for a second time.

They chose that day, a Sunday, to leave Jerusalem and fracture into two groups. We can conclude this logically without question. That gives yet another strong indication that the 36th day was when Jesus was put to death for a second time.

Another way that John is telling us that Jesus has returned from the dead a second time is how he reveals Jesus to us at the Sea of Tiberius. There is a dual role performed here by John and Peter that played out in the same fashion as in the previous chapter. John and Peter were the first apostles to joyfully discover that the tomb is empty, and were initially confused about what has happened, but then it was John who came to realize that Jesus had risen from the dead. In a similar fashion, it was John and Peter who were the first to see Jesus at the Sea of Tiberius after he had risen from the dead a second time, and again they were initially confused about what was going on with Jesus. Then, just like with the first resurrection, it was John who came to believe first, followed by Peter. Also note that the men run towards Christ just as they ran towards the empty tomb. The two scenes transpire in remarkably the same fashion. In fact this may be further evidence of the reverse order theory stated above. The mad dash by John and Peter to the empty tomb happens of course after the Last Supper, whereas this second discovery of Jesus occurs before the sacred breakfast. It is also unusual that the apostles have no trouble recognizing Jesus in the first two appearances, but for some reason they are unable to immediately recognize Him during the third appearance. Has he been somehow transformed by the second resurrection?

A second resurrection also fits in with a subtle theme that runs through John's gospel, namely how a number of key events happened twice. John the Baptist insists to his followers that he is not the messiah, that there is someone greater coming after him, "whose sandal strap I am not worthy to untie"[98] (John 1:26). Then he repeats this to his disciples in chapter three a second time by saying "you yourselves can testify that I said (that) I am not the Messiah, but that I was sent before him"[99] (John 3:28). Jesus performs his first miracle in Cana in chapter two when He turns water into wine, and then John has Him come back to that town to perform a second sign in Cana in chapter four when He heals the son of a royal official. "Now this was the second sign Jesus did when he came to Galilee from Judea"[100] (John 4:54). John also has two separate accounts of Christ curing on the Sabbath day. The first is in chapter five when Jesus tells a crippled man, "Rise, take up your mat and walk"[101] (John 5:8). The second cure on the Sabbath is in chapter nine when the messiah cures a man born blind by smearing clay into his eyes. It is also worth pointing out that when Jesus was arrested by a band of Jewish guards and Roman soldiers in chapter 18, this was in fact the second time according to John that troops were sent to arrest Him. The first occasion happened in chapter seven. "The Pharisees heard the crowd murmuring about him to this effect, and the chief priests and the Pharisees sent guards to arrest him"[102] (John 7:32). In the Gospels of Matthew, Mark, and Luke, Jesus makes one appearance in front of the Sanhedrin after being taken captive. By contrast in John's gospel, Jesus appears before the Sanhedrin on two separate occasions, once before Annas, and a second time in front of Caiaphas. "So the band of soldiers, the tribune, and the Jewish guards seized Jesus, bound him, and brought him to Annas first"[103] (John 18:13). As we have noted extensively as well, Jesus has two significant meals with His apostles, the Last Supper, and Primus Prandium. A second resurrection would fit in with this theme repeated here six separate times. One or two examples of key events happening twice would probably not even be worth noting, but six repeated events, especially of that magnitude, looks more like a distinct pattern.

Another question to ask is what happened between day seven, the time of the second appearance, and day 36, the date of the second death? That is 29 days that are unaccounted for. Certainly we can assume a few things. Christ was likely to have visited His mother at least once. St. Paul tells us He boldly appeared to a crowd of 500 witnesses as we mentioned earlier. I suspect that may have been a turning point during these intervening days. Think of the potential impact that would make. Logically that means 500 more voices to spread the word to all of their individual networks of friends and family members that Jesus of Nazareth was back from the dead. It would have been during those pivotal days that the Sanhedrin and Pilate would be getting increasingly nervous about the reports of this risen messiah. It would be during those pivotal days when Jesus would realize this renewed threat to Himself, His apostles, and His newly forming church. It would be during those pivotal days when He would be captured again and presumed dead, causing his followers to flee for their lives and finally give up on the dream of the Kingdom of God. It would be during those pivotal days when Jesus of Nazareth would show the world that He could conquer death a second time.

Another question we need to address is whether the Catholic Church covered up evidence of a second resurrection. Although there is no need to go over the entire history of the Council of Nicea, and the Council of Trent, the church certainly has selectively picked what to put in and out of the Bible. Was evidence of a second resurrection left out? If so, why? Having concluded that there is such strong evidence that Christ died, and rose from the dead a second time, we need to answer this question. If we look at the Gospel of John, it appears that there is a missing chapter between chapter 20 and chapter 21. There is a huge narrative gap there as we have exhaustively explained. Put simply, the apostles are commissioned to start the church in chapter 20, and then in the next scene, in chapter 21, they have immediately and completely given up, and also fractured apart for no apparent reason provided by the author. Can we conclude therefore that the Catholic Church removed whatever material existed between those two chapters, to hide evidence of a second resurrection? Building off what we previously stated, let us go a bit further with this. Chapter 20 ends seven days after the first resurrection. We also concluded above that the apostles must have left Jerusalem to make the journey to Galilee on the 36th day after the first resurrection. They then arrived in Galilee on the evening of the 39th day, and then witnessed Jesus' final appearance to them on the morning of the 40th day. That means that 29 days transpired between the end of chapter 20 and beginning of chapter 21. That is the vast majority of the 40 days Jesus spent on this earth after the first resurrection. That is almost 75% of that time that is unaccounted for. In other words, for some reason we are supposed to believe that Jesus' most favored apostle was unable to account for us almost three fourths of the post-resurrection time. This is counterintuitive. There is nothing near such a large and obvious chronological gap anywhere else in Gospel of John. It simply does not make any sense for John to leave this large amount of time unaccounted for. It is a huge, gaping narrative black hole. What makes this even more unusual is that John was alive during these days and would have known what Jesus was doing, especially if he was at least part of that time taking care of His mother, whom Jesus likely would have visited several times. It seems reasonable to conclude then that chapter 21 actually would have been chapter 22, and that the missing 21 contained the story of how Jesus was hunted down, executed, and rose from the dead a second time. I mentioned before how every major event in the Gospel of John happens in twos, so a 22nd chapter to end the gospel also makes better symbolic sense on that level as well.

Why would this be taken out of the gospel? What subversive purpose would it serve the church to cover this up? A story of a second resurrection would radically contradict the other gospels. Luke and Mark were not apostles so they would not have known about this, especially if this was just meant for Pontius Pilate and the apostles to know about. As for Matthew, he broke away from the group at some point after the second appearance, as evidenced by the fact that he did not go with the other apostles to Galilee, so he also may not have known about such an event as this. He also curiously has no knowledge of the Ascension either, so he may have been completely out of the picture in the last few weeks of Jesus' time on earth.

Therefore a story about a second resurrection that appeared only in one gospel would not fit the narrative of the other three. It could undermine the credibility and importance of the first resurrection, or perhaps even cast doubt on it. Having to explain to believers that Christ needed to rise from the dead a second time would be difficult to understand. Better to just edit that part out. The problem with doing that though, is that chapter 20 and chapter 21 make no logical sense when you read them back to back without an explanation of why the apostles gave up and fractured. The 29 days of missing time needs to be there to make what John wrote have even the resemblance of a logical and sequential narrative structure. One has to conclude that John would not have left that large amount of time unaccounted for. It would be irresponsible as an author. These were crucial days in the life of Jesus when He came back from the dead. Surely, something important must have transpired in the course of 29 days that he would have wanted to write about. If we can conclude that, then whatever he wrote must have been so controversial that it had to be removed from the gospel, otherwise it would have been left in. There would be no need to remove something like an account of Jesus appearing to other people, or visiting His mother. I do not think we ever will know who removed the missing chapter from the Gospel of John, when it took place, or why. What I am confident in saying though is that it makes no sense for John to leave a 29 day gap during some of the most crucial days Jesus spent on this earth after He came back from the dead. What John wrote we will never know, but the fact that it seems to have been deliberately removed leads me to believe that it was so controversial that it could not be included in the final version of the gospel. The only event that would rise to that level would be John's account of the second death and resurrection of Jesus Christ. Where is this account? Was it destroyed centuries ago at one of the church councils that determined what was going to be put in the Bible? Was it preserved by someone at the Vatican, and now sits buried deep within the Vatican archives, never to be seen again? Where is the missing chapter of the Gospel of John? We are likely never to know, nor get the Church to admit its existence. Absent their cooperation in the quest for the truth, it therefore becomes necessary for us to imagine based on the previous facts here assembled, how these momentous events may have transpired so many centuries ago.

Part Two

Hunting the Nazarene

Day 1: 8 a.m., Jerusalem

Mary Magdalene could not stop sobbing. The air was simply not entering her lungs long enough to produce words. This haggard, pathetic looking woman had appeared at Peter's door just as the sun was giving rise to another hellish day in Judea. Simon Peter was pleading with Mary to explain why she was so hysterical. Minutes seemed like hours until he could extract from her what was wrong.

"They have taken the Lord!"

John had just arrived at the door to see what all the fuss was about. He, like Peter, had just managed to fall back to sleep having tossed and turned all night, going over in his mind how they could go on without Jesus, how he had seen the master so brutally murdered just days before.

"Who would want to steal his body, and how could it even be done?" John asked, mostly to himself. Neither of them seemed to hear him anyway over the continued loud moaning of Mary. The best thing to do would be to investigate the matter, a thought that apparently occurred to Peter as well.

"We must see this for ourselves," said Simon Peter, heading out the door with John closely behind. The younger man caught up quickly and they both began to run as they got nearer to the entry point of the tomb. They were shocked to see the massive boulder pushed aside leaving a gaping hole. John glanced in and saw the burial clothes. Surprisingly, the smell of death was nowhere in the air. Peter went in and examined the tomb and thought it curious that the cloth that covered Jesus' head was rolled up in a separate area in the tomb.

"Why would they do that?" Peter thought out loud. John did not hear him, still lingering at the opening of the burial site.

"Come on in, John. What do you make of this?"

"He was not moved. This is not the work of a grave robber. Everything here is too orderly. Nothing has been stolen or broken," John pointed out.

"What then are you saying?"

"That we need to have faith," John said.

With that the two disciples left the tomb and headed back to the upper room. On the walk back Peter was even more afraid than ever.

"If they stole Jesus, we could be next. We need to stay hidden. Judas would have known what to do, what Christ was planning. We need to keep the doors locked tonight. No one will be allowed in," said Peter.

Day 1: 9 a.m., Jerusalem

Mary decided to stay at the tomb as Peter and John left. She had little strength to walk anywhere, having scarcely slept or ate anything since the nightmare that was Friday. Her mind was outside of time, existing only in the memories of her life with the only man she had ever loved, the man she called master and teacher. Now he was impossibly dead, and his beautiful, graceful body was missing. She thought that she might as well stay at the tomb because that is where she felt the closest to him anyway.

Then somewhere deep within her mind she heard a voice. Was it talking to her? There was brilliant light on her eyes which made it difficult to open them. The struggle was almost too much to bear for her dizzying brain, but sure enough there were two people now sitting in the master's tomb. One of them was indeed trying to talk to her. The voice was neither male nor female, just words that somehow she was hearing in her mind.

"Woman, why are you weeping?" they asked her. She said she was looking for Jesus but someone had stolen his body. Then another voice asked her the same question. Thinking it was the gardener she pleaded with him to tell her where the body had been taken.

"Mary!" came the reply from Jesus.

Mary threw herself to her knees and grabbed Jesus' garments, needing to touch Him to assuage her grief. "Teacher!" she said to

Him, now crying again in her utter joy at seeing Him.

Jesus wanted to linger with her longer but there was so much more of His Father's work to be done on this day.

"Please stop holding onto me, for I have not yet ascended to the Father. I will soon be going to my Father who is your Father, who is my God and who is your God. Tell this to Peter and the others. As difficult as it is for us to leave each other now, I promise I will see you again soon," Jesus said.

Mary released Him from her grasp and ran back to where this morning had begun. This time though when she reached the house where the apostles were hiding she was not crying, but shouting instead. The door was locked. She began pounding on it.

"Simon Peter! Simon Peter! Unlock the door! It is Mary!"

Hearing that familiar voice outside, Peter raced downstairs, thinking Mary perhaps discovered who had taken Jesus. He unlocked the door, but before he could ask her what she found out she burst into the house running up the stairs, tripping over her own garments, bellowing the news, "I have seen the Lord!"

Day 1: 9 a.m., Jerusalem, Sanhedrin council chambers

The guards were in a state of panic. It was difficult for the chief priests to understand exactly what they were saying because these men were talking over each other in loud bursts of noise. The youngest of the group was completely incoherent, just holding himself tightly as if needing protection from some unseen threat.

"Silence," said Caiaphas, the high priest, pounding his staff on the ground for emphasis. The guard quieted themselves and formed a line out of respect for their employer.

"One at a time. What has happened?"

"The Nazarene is no longer dead. We have seen this with our own eyes," said the captain of the guard.

"Surely this cannot be true," said Annas, another of the high priests.

"The King of the Jews lives," the guard said. "We all saw him leave the tomb. Anyone who tells you differently would be lying to you. You need to understand that he walks among us again."

"Remain here," said Caiaphas.

The priests then held a private counsel to determine what to do next.

"If this is true, then he is now an even greater threat. We need to keep this word from spreading. We can take no chances with this man, and his followers," said Annas.

"The guards will help us spread the rumor that his body was stolen," said Caiaphas. "This will give us enough time to formulate another plan to take care of this threat."

The guards were then paid to spread the rumor that Jesus' body was stolen during the night, and with that they quietly shuffled out of the chambers, with only the sound of their armor filling the eerie void. For a long while Annas and Caiaphas remained silent, searching for answers that were not coming. Then the high priest looked up into the grey eyes of his aging counterpart.

"We need to pay another visit to the governor," said Caiaphas.

Day 1: 9 p.m., Jerusalem

All day long the arguments were raging back and forth. At one point Andrew even had Peter pinned up against the wall. Brothers often fight, but this was something different. Something personal.

"Your lack of faith has me questioning your leadership. If Mary says the Lord has returned, then it is true. Jesus himself said he would restore the Kingdom of God in three days. This is now the third day. He is back from the dead. He has conquered death itself," said Andrew.

"Then where is he? Why does he not appear to us? We have been waiting all these hours here, scared for our lives. Surely he must know we are suffering here."

Peter had instructed James to be on guard. He and a few of the others were taking shifts watching the windows for any sign of the Sanhedrin. Nathanael had passed out in exhaustion in the corner having just completed his shift of relentlessly pacing back and forth near the windows.

"Our suffering and fear is nothing compared to what he went through," John said. "I alone among you watched him on the cross as his own mother saw his tortured body collapse into death."

"I wish Judas was here," said Philip. "He always knew what Jesus was going to do. The two of them were always planning and conspiring together. He could tell us what to expect."

"What we can expect is that we will be running out of food soon," Simon pointed out, picking at some bread. "We cannot stay up here forever."

The mood grew even tenser as the hours crept toward twilight, with Jude and John arguing over just what kind of messiah Jesus was meant to be. No one could agree on anything this night, expect for one thing.

"If you keep shouting at one another, surely we will be found to be hiding here," Matthew said, forcing his way into the middle of the room. "I want everyone to come to the center of the room and sit down."

No one moved.

"Yes, everyone please wash and sit down," said Peter. Slowly the men got up from where they were scattered about the room, and did as they were instructed, forming a circle in the center of the room.

"What bread do we have left?" Peter asked.

"Just this small loaf," said Simon, giving it to Peter.

Instinctively the men took a piece and passed it around to each other, as well as some wine that Philip had brought into the circle.

"Let us then pray as Jesus taught us," said Peter. The eleven men then lowered their heads, and closed their eyes instinctively, but the air in the room shifted somehow. Before anyone could speak they heard a familiar voice.

"Peace be with you."

The apostles all opened their eyes to behold the son of God, risen from the dead. They stumbled upon one another to be the first to touch His hands and His side, rejoicing that their master had returned to them. It was a moment that left ten men literally speechless. Words were not needed at this moment in time. All that was needed was existence, to stand within the presence of this man, to behold Him, to smell Him, to love Him.

Jesus then began to smile and speak once again, "Peace be with you, as the Father has sent me so I send you." Still quietly watching and obeying His every word, the master instructed the men to form a circle once again, as He went slowly from one to another breathing onto them and saying, "Receive the Holy Spirit, whose sins you forgive are forgiven, whose sins you retain are retained."

"We are ready, my Lord to serve you, and the Father, with the power of the Holy Spirit," said Peter.

"I will be with you only a short time before I must ascend to my Father, but the Father is with you, and I am with you as you preach the coming of the Kingdom of God."

With that Jesus left them with a promise to return.

"What do we do now?" asked Andrew to his brother.

"Unlock the door."

Day 2: 7 p.m., home of Pontius Pilate

It had been another long day for the Roman governor. He did not enjoy ordering the death of someone, but He came to view it as just another aspect of this increasingly unpleasant job. As he tried to explain over the cloying protestations of his wife, the guards had simply not performed their duty to secure the tomb.

Refusing to execute them would set a bad example among the ranks. Worse yet, these men might go around spreading foolish rumors that the Nazarene had risen from the dead. They needed to be silenced and punished.

Increasingly, the only things to look forward to these days were the late night meals. There were some perks to being governor and they came in the form of lamb, fresh bread, and some cheese. Pilate was just about to tear off his first piece of hot roasted flesh, when the voice of his attendant intruded into his solitude like the bone he almost caught in his throat.

"The Sanhedrin is here."

"All of them?" asked Pilate.

"No, just two," said the guard.

"Then why did you not say that to begin with?" he said furiously, and with a flourish threw down his piece of lamb onto the floor.

"Now pick that up," he told the guard.

The man did as he was instructed, and began to bend over to grab it, but the master had other ideas for his prey.

"No. On your hands and knees."

Seeing the filth that was now on the ragged piece of flesh, the guard knew what was next.

"Stay down there and put that in your mouth to quiet the stupidity that flows from it."

The man did as he was told, and like an animal trained to obey on command, he forced the dirt laden piece into his mouth and swallowed hard.

"Get up and show them in, if that is within your limited capabilities."

Pilate was having fun now, and had a smile on his face when Annas and Caiaphas entered his private chambers.

"We apologize for intruding on your grace at this late hour," said Annas.

"And we regret that we have apparently interrupted your

meal," noted Caiaphas.

"It is of no consequence," said Pilate. "I had little hope for a peaceful end to this day anyway so your presence here is likely to do nothing but improve my mood."

Pilate then realized why they were there and suddenly grew even more hopeful that he could resume his meal before the meat got cold. He could have these Jews gone in a few minutes.

"I know why you here," Pilate said, now being a bit coy. He liked to have the upper hand with these men to keep them in their place.

"It is about the guards assigned to secure the tomb of your King of the Jews." He felt certain that term would annoy them.

"Yes, that is correct your grace," said Annas.

"I knew it!" Pilate said, with a satisfied laugh as he clapped his hands. "Rest assured the matter has been taken care of. They were executed earlier today for dereliction of duty."

"Executed!" said Annas.

"Yes, isn't that what you are here for, to ensure that they were punished?"

"No. We are more concerned about what they said before they died," said Caiaphas. "We have spent most of this day trying to confirm this, and it seems that what they reported may in fact be true."

"Surely you are not referring to the idea that your King of the Jews has risen from the dead," Pilate said mockingly.

"That is precisely what I am saying, and the three of us would be wise to look into this matter further. If this is true then it will be the end for all of us," said Caiaphas.

"Remember where you are and who you are speaking to," Pilate snorted back at him.

"It is precisely because I know who I am speaking to that I warn you of this renewed threat," the high priest said.

"We cannot afford to let this man make fools of us, nor his followers," said Annas.

Suddenly Pilate remembered what his wife said about the fate of his soul, and how he had washed his hands of all this.

"I need to reflect on what the best course of action is here," said the governor. "Let us not do anything just yet. Come back in a week and will we decide then on an appropriate course of action."

"As you wish, governor," said Caiaphas.

After the two men left, Pilate was in for one final intrusion on his evening meal plans. This one he did not have the pleasure of ignoring. Her haggard appearance meant only one thing. Another sleepless night filled with her so-called "visions."

"What is it now, Claudia? More bad dreams?" Pilate said his best derisive tone.

"Who was that?" she asked him, pulling tight her robe to cover her exposed cleavage.

"Just the Sanhedrin," he said, settling back at the table with renewed hope of devouring his now-cold meat.

"I dreamed about him again," she said, pulling her arms in tight to brace herself from the chilly evening air. "You are going to see him again. He said to me that his Father has more work for him to do."

Pilate looked up from his food, and noticed that wife was now shivering. It gave him pause and all he could think to dumbly say was, "Are you cold?"

"No. I am afraid."

Day 3: 6 p.m., Nazareth, home of Mary, mother of Jesus

She had been keeping herself busy, trying to will the image of her dying son out of her mind. There was nothing for her any more in Jerusalem. She made good time, completing the journey back home to Nazareth in four days.

Idleness had never been her way of life, since she was a young girl. Mary prided herself on the meticulous weaving and embroidering that her mother Anne had taught her. She was the first girl in her village who could majestically balance a jar on her head, which she found herself doing again this evening. It was an especially dusty and warm end to the day, so she felt like bringing back some fresh water from the well to the house.

As Mary began the sharp ascent up the path to the two room dwelling she had called home for so many years, she heard the thin curtain covering the front door snapping sharply in the breeze. She thought to herself that it would probably be a good night to sleep on the roof because of the cooling breeze.

As she entered the house she put the water jug down on the floor, spilling some on the carpet. Mary instinctively grabbed a rag to sop up the excess wetness. She kneeled down and reached out, but before she could move any further a hand tenderly grasped her fingers. She turned with a violent start to see her son standing before her.

"Peace be with you."

Mary looked at him and initially she could not speak, still grasping the cloth in her hand as if it were her only connection to reality. Soon the joy began to overtake her emotions as she stood and enveloped herself within the safety of His arms.

"And with you, my son," Mary said. "Look at what they have done to you."

"It is the will of my Father," he said.

"I have been in utter despair these past few days, but I knew you would return," she said.

"Your faith has kept you strong," Jesus said. "But know, woman, that there is so much more of my Father's work to do."

"Well for now your Father's work requires you to eat," said his mother, eliciting the first smile she had seen from Him in months.

Mother and son spent the rest of the evening sharing a meal of bread, fish, and lentils before heading to the roof to sleep under the stars. Mary knew her son was a restless and fitful sleeper since he was a young boy. Tonight would be no different.

At 3 a.m. she found him standing at the edge of the roof murmuring prayers to His Father.

"What is bothering you, Jesus?"

"Evil is all around us. I am afraid for my disciples. I can sense their fear."

Mary said nothing. She knew there were times when she did not need to speak. Perhaps she already knew what he was going to say. She was afraid he was going to say the same frightening words he spoke to her just a few weeks ago. He did.

"There will be a great deal more suffering and sacrifice before I return to my Father."

Day 7: 9 p.m., Jerusalem, upper room

The peace Jesus gave to His apostles had not lasted even a week. A few like Peter and James had entered the streets at night with the intention of spreading the word that the messiah had returned from the dead, but fear quickly overcame their pointless efforts. Each of these aimless secret sorties sent the men scurrying back to the tenuous safety of the upper room where Christ had appeared to them after His resurrection. The Sanhedrin seemed to be lurking around every dark corner, watching their every move, or so it seemed. Not a single one of the eleven men knew how to begin this enormous task without getting killed. This fear was tearing the apostles apart.

"What good are we to the master if we are dead?" said Matthew. Being a tax collector, Matthew was always one of the most logical and reasonable of the disciples, consistently adept at getting to the salient point in any argument.

"We should all be willing to die for Him, as he died for us," said Jude.

"That is true, but He soon will ascend to the Father, and count on us to build His church," Matthew said, his tone rising. "Peter!"

Simon Peter was not paying attention, his focus trained on the window, apparently scanning for some unseen assassin lurking in the murky streets that wound outside their two story consistory.

"What is it Matthew?" Peter said rather meekly, making his way to the center of the room.

"We were just talking about building Jesus' church. Surely you of all people would know the importance of this." Matthew was getting angry, especially because Peter said nothing back.

"You have nothing to say?"

Peter nodded his head and went back to the window. What happened next though made Matthew even more incensed.

"I don't believe anything you are saying," said Thomas.

"You should, the Lord visited us here just seven days hence," said Matthew.

"If Jesus had returned from the dead, you men would not be hiding up here like the scared sheep that you are," said Thomas. "You tell me that you have seen the Lord, but I will not believe Jesus has risen from the dead unless I see the mark of the nails in his hands and put my fingers into the nailmarks and put my hand into his side. Only then will I believe."

"Peace be with you," said the familiar voice of their savior, followed by the sound of eleven men gasping and turning towards the door.

"It is the Lord!" cried out John, who ran to Him first to receive His embrace.

"Thomas, come here my son. Put your finger here and see my hands, and bring your hand and put it into my side, and do not be unbelieving but believe."

Thomas did as he was told, keeping his eyes closed as the master guided his hands over the marks of His crucifixion. Thomas opened his eyes and gazed directly into the eyes of his savior.

"My Lord and my God," was all he could manage to say in his humility.

"Have you come to believe because you have seen me?" said

Christ. Thomas nodded in shame. "Blessed are those who have not seen and have believed."

The apostles had now gathered around the master, listening intently.

"This will now be your mission, to build a church of believers, who have faith to believe without having seen."

"How can we do this, Lord?" said John. "We fear for our lives, and for your life too."

"Remember I have given you peace. Remember I have given you the blessing of my Father. Remember I have given you the gift of the Holy Spirit. Do not be afraid. You walk with the Kingdom of my Father, you speak with the power of the Holy Spirit, and you will perform signs in my name. Now you are fishers of men, and it is time to cast your nets into the world."

With that Jesus left them again, with instructions for John to return to Nazareth, and a promise to return soon.

None of the apostles dared to speak. They all felt the shame that Christ had to visit them a second time. Out of deference to his authority, the other ten men waited for the leader to speak. With their attention focused on him, Peter straightened his back, stroked his slightly graying beard, and swallowed hard to make ready his voice.

"In the morning, we begin again," said Peter. "No one is to stay in this room any longer. We will go where we are welcome and eat where we are welcome, like when we traveled with the master. This is how we will start. We will go two by two as the master sent us, so I send all of you."

"They may kill us all, and probably start with you, my brother," said Andrew.

"I suspect Jesus has a plan to stop that from happening," said John.

"What plan?" said Andrew. "How would I not know about it?"

"I am not sure, but He always finds a way to protect us, even if it would mean that He would have to die for us again."

Day 8: 3 a.m., Garden of Gethsemane

It was here that the Son felt closest to the Father. It was here that He could be at one with His Father's voice. Few words needed to be spoken on this sacred ground. Jesus placed His hands on the trunks of every tree that He passed, like greeting an old friend. He could feel the life coursing through these fig and olive branches that had stood as silent witnesses to His arrest just one week ago. Seeing the bounty and beauty of His Father's creations always gave Him sustenance.

Christ then knelt down, feeling the damp ground on His knees. The air was still and vacant, utterly absent of noise, while the continuity of time and space became distorted as the Son of God began speaking to His Father.

"Abba, you have led me to this ground to hear your voice. Fill my heart with not my will but your own. I have seen the fear in the eyes of my apostles. I fear for their lives. How can I protect them and show them the way?"

Jesus could then see in His mind a vision of Himself on a mountain speaking to hundreds of people. The answer was clear. He needed to show the apostles by His own example that there was nothing to fear. It was time to show Himself to anyone who would listen, and what better place than right here on the Mount of Olives?

Day 8: 6 p.m., Mount of Olives

By the time evening had arrived, word was spreading in the streets of Jerusalem that Jesus was in Gethsemane. At first dozens, and then hundreds followed Him up the side of the Mount of Olives, marveling at His scars and declaring Him the messiah. As many as five hundred were ready to hear Him speak.

"Peace be with you. So the Father has sent me, so I send you. I will be with you only a short time before I ascend to my Father on this very ground. There is still much more of my Father's work to be done. Although people have eyes they do not see. Although people have ears they do not hear. Open your eyes, and listen with your ears my children. Behold the lamb of God who has taken away the sins of the world. Amen, amen, I say to you blessed are those who proclaim the lamb of God in the face of persecution, for yours is the kingdom of God."

Jesus then began to descend the mountain, slowly making His way through the crowd. As He walked further down the hill He allowed His garments to fall freely from His body, leaving Himself completely nude. Many onlookers began gasping and crying, while a few women fainted at the site of His mangled frame.

Like He did with Thomas, Jesus knew it was important for these many disbelievers to see the lashings that had eviscerated His back, the gaping nail marks in His wrists, and the piercing of His side. The utter grotesqueness of His naked body was a graceful, yet awe-inspiring living testimony to the suffering He had endured for His people. It would be this stark image that these men and women would remember, more than the brief words He had spoken. The image of the crucified Christ would be their constant memory as they gave witness to the Kingdom of God.

Day 13: 6 p.m., Jerusalem

Immediately after Jesus left them for a second time, Peter had ordered the apostles to head out in groups of two as the master instructed them after all 13 were rejected at Nazareth over two years ago. All of the men remembered that assignment as their first real test of whether they could endure this austere life of following this man whom they had just recently met. It would be this experience that they would draw from to once again perform signs in His name.

With John back in Jesus' hometown taking care of Mary, and Judas dead, that left five groups of two to begin this sacred work.

Peter would go with his brother Andrew, while James would set out with his brother John. The same would go for Jude and the younger James who were brothers as well. Peter told Thomas to head out with Nathanael, while Matthew was paired up with Simon. Peter instructed them not to make any grand speeches, but instead to go quietly from house to house, and shake off the dust from the places where they were rejected.

It was now the Sabbath once again and Peter was in the mood to stir some things up like the master had done on this same miraculous ground earlier in His ministry. Christ had performed miracles on the Sabbath so Andrew suggested that they try to do the same thing. They were near the gate at the northeast wall of the temple area in Jerusalem where the animals were brought in for sacrifice. Near this gate were two pools said to heal the sick with its intermittently bubbling water. Bethesda, as it came to be known, was where Jesus healed a crippled man with only His words.

As Peter and Andrew approached the pool they could see almost a hundred or so anguished souls pushed into misery by their crippling diseases. Few even bothered to notice these two fishermen standing in their midst, as they surveyed this wretched landscape of mangled humanity.

"Where do we begin?" asked Andrew.

"They will choose for us," said Peter.

"How?"

"It must first be their faith that heals them as we speak through Christ," said Peter.

Peter placed himself directly in the middle of these men and women right near the entrance to the pools to position himself so that he could be heard by as many people as possible.

"My brother Andrew and I are here to proclaim the risen Lord, Jesus of Nazareth," said Peter. No one stirred, or even seemed to hear him.

"The kingdom of God is at hand," said Andrew. "Jesus of

Nazareth has risen from the dead. The Lord Jesus is your salvation."

"On this ground the Lord Jesus healed a crippled man," said Peter. "You as well may be healed through the power of the Lord Jesus."

This got their attention. Many began to sit up, or turn their bodies toward Peter and his brother.

"Throughout our three years with the Lord, we saw Him perform many signs in the name of His divine Father," Peter said. "Can anyone tell me how Jesus healed that crippled man on this very ground? Was it the water here that healed him?"

Peter dramatically put his hands into the pool and filled them with a small pool of water.

"No," said a frail looking woman. "It was not the water. The water is not what will heal me, or anyone else here."

"Then what will be your salvation?" said Peter.

There was a pause; a stillness in the air as everyone waited for her response. The continuity of space and time became distorted as Peter closed his eyes to position his savior into the center of his mind. His concentration was complete, as heat rose in his spine, stiffening his posture.

"The risen Lord Jesus," she said. "He is my salvation."

With that Peter opened his eyes and violently threw the water onto the ground, as if repulsed by its very presence on his hands.

"Get up and walk," said Peter. "Your faith has healed you. Never return to this place."

With that, the woman got up and wound her way through the maze of stunned onlookers.

Day 15: 10 p.m., Jerusalem, Sanhedrin Council chambers

What Peter and Andrew failed to realize was that the Sanhedrin had been tracking their movements in the last several days, waiting to arrest them for violating Jewish law.

"We have it on good authority that the man they call Simon

Peter, one of Jesus' disciples healed a crippled woman on the Sabbath," said Annas.

"This man is the appointed leader of the followers of Jesus," said Caiaphas. "He must be taken in for questioning. This must be done quietly so as not to incite a riot."

"The followers of the Nazarene are growing daily," said Annas. "It will be difficult to arrest him without causing a scene. We need to be careful about whatever course of action we take and the effect it will produce."

"Agreed," said Caiaphas. "He will be brought in tomorrow night under the protection of a small Roman guard that I will procure from the governor."

Day 21: 11 p.m., Jerusalem, Sanhedrin Council Chambers

When Peter was arrested it came as no surprise to him. He was ready for the Jewish high priests to take him into custody. It was just a matter time. The only thing that was a bit unusual was that it took this long to happen. He and his brother had spent much of their time since the Sabbath going house to house in Jerusalem doing much the same work they did on that day. Most Jews rejected them outright, which forced them to quickly move on to other areas outside of the city in some cases. Now they both were back in the holy city, but under completely different circumstances.

"Are you the one they call Simon Peter?" asked Annas.

"You know who I am," said Peter. "This is my brother Andrew, but I am sure you already know that too. Why have we been brought here?"

"I will be the one asking the questions," said Annas.

Peter looked over at his brother, and caught a glimpse of him smiling at him. Andrew was enjoying Peter's rocklike fortitude. His brother had always been emotional, but this was something new.

"Are you the leader of the followers of Jesus?" asked Caiaphas.

"So you have said," answered Peter. "Our only leader is the risen Lord Jesus."

"It has come to our attention that you and your brother healed a crippled woman on the Sabbath," said Caiaphas. "Do you deny this accusation?"

"Even if I denied such an accusation the Sanhedrin would only choose to believe the testimony of its own informants," said Peter.

Peter shot a warning glance over to Andrew who had his hand to mouth, stifling a laugh.

"You and your brother would be wise to cease your current course of action," said Annas, now looking directly at Andrew. "If we find you preaching about your risen Lord or breaking Jewish law again there will be serious consequences. You would be better off going back to Galilee and resuming your lives as fishermen."

"Jesus has made us fishers of men," said Andrew. "And that is what we always will be. We cannot go back. The master has forbidden it."

"Think carefully what you do. You will be monitored by this council over the period of the next two weeks. You are to report to the governor's palace on that day for possible sentencing," said Caiaphas.

As Peter and Andrew left the chambers they could not help but be in a sullen mood, overcome with more feelings of fear and dejection.

"I know what we need to do," said Andrew.

"What?" said Peter.

"We need to go to Nazareth."

Day 25: 6 p.m., Nazareth, house of Mary, mother of Jesus

The trek from Jerusalem to Nazareth had been a four day nightmare. On the second day, a small group of bandits stopped the two brothers, but seeing they had little of value, allowed them to pass without incident. Although no one got hurt, it shook both of them enough to know that they could have been killed on the spot. On the third day, Andrew was gashed in the left forearm while fending off a small mountain lion. The two men managed to chase away the wild beast with their walking sticks after Peter clubbed the animal in the head.

When they reached Nazareth both men were exhausted, dehydrated, and coated in a film of grime. It had been so long since they had been to Jesus' hometown, that it took some time to get acclimated enough to make their way to Mary's hillside home. As they approached the house the sound of John's raucous, boyish laughter was unmistakable. Given that it was such a warm evening, Peter expected to find Jesus, John, and Mary on the roof, and sure enough that is where they found them. Actually it was the master who did the finding first.

"Simon Peter! Andrew!" shouted Jesus. "We are up here enjoying some wine. Will you join us my brothers?"

"Certainly, my Lord!" replied Peter.

The two men entered the house and put down their bags before climbing the ladder to take in the musky evening air. With now five people on the roof, Peter looked around a bit precariously. Mary seemed to know what he was thinking.

"My husband Joseph built this roof and this house with his own hands," said Mary. "There is nothing to fear."

"He was the best carpenter in all of Nazareth," said Jesus. "He was a great teacher who had enormous patience for his son."

The mood had suddenly turned somber with the talk of the dead, so Peter had to wait to broach the subject of why they had made this journey. The master seemed to sense the growing anxiety within Simon Peter, so Christ broke off the conversation to confront him about the purpose of their visit.

"What is bothering you, my friend?" said Jesus. "Why have you and Andrew made this trip? Please tell all of us what has happened."

"As you instructed, the apostles have all gone into the world to spread the news of your resurrection. I sent them out two by two, but we have been met with resistance," said Peter.

"What kind of resistance?" asked Jesus.

"From Pilate and the Sanhedrin," answered Andrew. "We have been accused of breaking sacred law by healing as you did on the Sabbath."

"The high priests have given us 11 more days to stop preaching and go back to Galilee," said Peter. "We wanted to make you aware of this threat to the building of your church here on earth."

"My Kingdom has been established in heaven for the forgiveness of sins through my death and resurrection," said Jesus. "Now we need to establish a kingdom on earth for the glory of God."

"We are frightened," said Peter.

"There is much to fear," said Jesus "But my Father's will can be done even through death. Now eat, drink and spend the night here. In the morning please return to Jerusalem."

"What are you going to do?" asked Peter. "What are we supposed to do?"

"Try to have faith.' Jesus said.

With that everyone left the roof to turn in for the night, except for Jesus. One thought entered His mind, the solution to His problems.

He needed to return to Gethsemane.

Day 29: 1 a.m., Gethsemane

The air was sweet and crisp, as Jesus made his descent into Gethsemane, once again finding Himself among His old confederates. The gnarled branches of the olive and fig trees seemed like long inviting arms, offering Christ the slumbering embrace of a trusted friend. Jesus decided to lay down near the trunk of the tree with the lowest hanging branches, and quickly found

Himself falling asleep under this makeshift awning. It was easy to see how the apostles had given into the same impulse on the night of the Passover meal.

As the son of God drifted into sleep, He began to commune with His Father. The Son was telling the Father that the lives of the apostles were being threatened, and because of this His kingdom on earth was being threatened as well. Jesus then saw a vision of Himself suffering more at the hands of the Romans.

"Is this your will, Abba? That I trade my life for theirs; that I suffer to protect them?"

Jesus knew the answer. He would have to die again to save them. He would show those who would harm His church that He truly was the Son of God with a direct display of the divine power of the Holy Spirit, who will give Him new life, born again like His baptism from John so many years ago.

As Jesus woke up, as the sun was coming up in the eastern sky, He realized that several hours had passed since He fell asleep. The Holy Spirit began speaking to Him to comfort His anxiety about what lay ahead for Him in the coming days. Jesus vocalized these sacred thoughts and heard Himself say, "no one has greater love than this, to lay down one's life for one's friends."

Day 30: 6 p.m., Jerusalem, home of Pontius Pilate

"The Nazarene has made fools of all of us," said Pilate. "You can deny all you want that He is not back from the dead, but the reality is that we have made Him more powerful by killing him."

"We have made plans to get rid of His followers," said Annas. "They have six more days to leave Jerusalem."

"Why not just force them to leave immediately, or just kill them now?" asked the governor.

"Their support among the people is growing, so we need to seem fair in our dealings with these followers so as not to incite a riot," said Caiaphas. "If they refuse to leave we will have legal justification to execute them at that point."

"And as for Jesus what plans do you have for him?" Pilate asked.

"He must be executed as well. His crimes against Rome and his blasphemous behavior are still enough to put him to death a second time," said Annas. "None of that has changed."

"Agreed," Pilate said. "He must be hunted down and killed to put an end to this continued threat to peace, and order. We must erase this man and his followers from everyone's collective memory. If he is proven to be the messiah, then our decision to kill the son of God will ruin all of us."

"There is still time to make sure that does not happen," said Caiaphas

"We must act quickly to find this man and put him to death," said Annas.

"You have my full support," said Pilate. "I will dispatch some of our best guards here to accompany you when you attempt to arrest him."

"Your grace, may I offer a word of advice?" said Annas.

"What advice could I possibly want from you?" said Pilate.

"We know the preferred method of Roman execution is crucifixion," said Annas. "We would like to suggest that method not be used this time, given its failure to produce its intended results."

"A different method of execution needs to be attempted this time with constant watch over the body until we are satisfied that He is not returning from the dead. We need to think of a powerful method of execution."

Looking over at the large reflecting pools in his portico, Pilate began to smile.

"I'm sure we could think of something."

Day 30: 6 p.m., home of Mary Magdalene, Galilee

Their embrace was difficult to end for both of them. She had not seen Him in a month, and it seemed now every time she was in

His presence she could do nothing but cry. Mary had mourned so deeply to the very depths of her sanity when He died, and rejoiced like a child when He returned. Now "the teacher" was back again, and she could only hope He would linger in her arms for hours.

"I have missed you so deeply," she said, "yet I know I must not take you away from your Father's work."

"I have missed you as well, my dearest Mary," said Jesus, as He began to detach Himself from her blue robe. "You are unique among my disciples in the special bond that we have always shared. I want you to be part of building my Father's kingdom here on earth, just like all of the other disciples who have followed me."

"Why do you say this to me now, my Lord?" asked Mary.

"Because I shall be ascending to my Father in nine days and I fear for the lives of the apostles," said Jesus. "It is you who can do my Father's will on this earth long after I am gone, and long after the apostles meet their fate. I will be counting on you."

Jesus was reluctant to continue this conversation with Mary, because He knew how she of all people was going to react to what He was going to tell her next.

"I wanted you to be the first to know that my Father's will is that I need to suffer more for the sake of my disciples, and for the safety of His kingdom here on earth," said Jesus.

"Surely you have suffered enough," said Mary. "Surely there must be another way."

"This is my Father's will and I must do as He wants," said Jesus. "I do not know what is going to happen to me, but I know I will see you again one day in paradise in my Father's kingdom in heaven."

Surprisingly there were no tears from Mary. No sobbing, or weeping. She seemed to except this fate for her master. It would do no good to further attempt to talk him out of whatever plan had already been set in motion for Himself, and the forces conspiring against Him.

"I wish I could come with you," Mary said, "to share this pain with you, and take some of its burden from your shoulders."

"That is not necessary," said Jesus. "I already have someone in mind who will be accompanying me to Jerusalem to confront those who would destroy my church."

"I think John is an excellent selection to go with you," said Mary, with a wry smile.

Jesus was taken aback by her clairvoyance, but could not help but return the smile with one of his own. As he had told her, they always did have a special bond that even death could never break.

Day 32: 6 a.m., Nazareth, home of Mary, mother of Jesus

Jesus arrived early so as not to awaken His mother. This would be hard enough to explain to John, let alone His own mother. Jesus Himself was not exactly sure what awaited Him this time in Jerusalem, only that more suffering was ahead. He would need John to report back to the apostles what had happened to Him, whatever that might be.

The plan was to head directly to Pilate who would then presumably call upon the Sanhedrin to join him in his private quarters. Jesus knew they still wanted Him dead. That much had not changed. He wondered if they knew that He also wanted to die. This was the one concern Jesus had. What if they refused to put Him to death? This must be done willingly for all parties involved. So much remained unknown. He must have faith and trust in the will of his Father. This much was certain, Christ was not going to allow the Sanhedrin any chance to execute Peter and the other apostles. He would trade His life for theirs.

"Wake up, son of thunder," Jesus said to John. "A new day awaits."

"Master!"

Fortunately John was sleeping on the floor, and Mary was on the roof so she did not hear him.

"Stay quiet, my child. I do not wish to awaken my mother," said Jesus. "Gather your supplies. A long journey lies ahead."

"Where are we going, my Lord?"

"To Jerusalem."

John was confused. He knew how much danger, and how many of Jesus' enemies filled that ancient city.

"Surely somewhere safer would be more prudent, master?"

Jesus stood silently, regarding John, thinking how much he had grown and matured in the last three years since He had first called upon him in Galilee.

"My Father's will awaits us there, and it will be for you to tell the others what happens to me, no matter how difficult that may be."

"It shall be done."

"As shall the will of the Father for His only Son," Jesus said as He lovingly ran His fingers through John's hair.

Day 36: 12:30 a.m., Jerusalem, home of Pontius Pilate

As they drew closer to Jerusalem, Jesus decided that He did not want John to witness what was about to happen to Him, whatever that might be once they reached Pilate's home. He needed to do this alone. John had already given Him what He needed most, walking side by side with Him, giving Jesus his faith and trust to help Him see this through to the bitter end. Christ knew that John had already suffered enough seeing Him die the first time. Another concern was that the same forces out to get Him, might decide to kill John too. It would be better to simply have John report back to the apostles that He had been arrested. He wanted to test their faith, and John would be the one to deliver the message to them.

"Your journey ends here, my child."

"But we have not entered yet, master," John protested. "I wish to stay with you by your side until the end."

"I need you to do something else instead."

"What is it, my Lord?" said John.

"You are to report to Simon Peter not to come here today," said Jesus. "That I have been arrested and taken into custody by the Jews and Pilate."

John seemed apprehensive.

"Tell them that this is the will of my Father, and you have merely done what I have instructed you to do, that I am here of my own free will."

John was beginning to sob, as he began to say in broken words, "What," he said, "will become of you, master?"

"It is for the Father to decide," Jesus said. "Go now and do as I say."

John then kissed Jesus, and ran into the night.

Their conversation had aroused the ire of the half sleeping Roman guard monitoring the grounds outside of Pilate's residence. They quickly grabbed Jesus and brought Him inside. He looked directly into their eyes.

"You are to take me to see the governor immediately," Jesus said.

There was a flutter of recognition in the eyes of the guards that then turned into panic. All they could muster was to dumbly say, "Yes."

The three of them walked down a narrow corridor. The sounds of the boots of these two massive men in armor clanking off the marble floor provided an eerie echo in the darkness.

"Wait here," the older one said. "We will rouse the governor."

Jesus then kneeled and turned His back to the hallway that the guards had walked down, and began to pray.

"Father, if there is some other way, please tell me now, but not my will but yours fill my heart in my time of need."

What Jesus did not know was that Pilate had invited Caiaphas and Annas to spend the night inside his palace. They expected Peter and Andrew to arrive in the morning, so Pilate felt that in the spirit of governmental efficiency, the three of them could rule on their fate immediately when they arrived. So it was surprising to all of them when Jesus turned around to see not just Pilate, but Annas and Caiaphas as well.

"All hail the King of the Jews!" Annas said mockingly.

"So you say," said Jesus.

"The son of God has returned," said Caiaphas. "You apparently were not dead the first time we tried to kill you. We will not make the same mistake again."

"That is not your decision to make," said Pilate. "This man has done nothing wrong. I am reluctant to get involved again with this decision to execute an innocent man."

"This is a matter for the Jews," said Annas.

"Anything that threatens law and order pertains to me," said Pilate. "You have involved me with this matter from the very beginning and I will see it through to the end. You have no one to blame but yourself for Roman involvement."

The chief priests stayed quiet, suddenly remembering where they were.

"I know that you want my disciples to leave Jerusalem, or face execution," said Jesus. "I know that they are to report here today to face banishment, or execution. I have a solution that will satisfy everyone here."

"We are listening," said Caiaphas.

"Kill me instead," said Jesus. "Take my life and prove that I am not the son of God. If I rise from the dead, you will have no choice but to leave my apostles alone and allow them to preach the word of God in these streets. If the three of you do not witness my resurrection here, then you will prove me to be a fake. Peace, order, and your credibility will be restored."

"I cannot make promises for them," said Pilate, "but if you demonstrate this to me, I will do nothing to stop your apostles from preaching, as long as I am governor. My wife wants her nightmares to come to an end, and so do I. Demonstrate this to us right here, son of God, and I will do as you say."

"If he is to be killed here," said Annas. "We want the body constantly monitored to assure us that He is dead."

"Of course," said Pilate. "I will personally see to it."

"My new life began in the sacred waters of John who baptized me," said Jesus. "That is where it shall end here this morning."

"Then place yourself in this large pool," said Pilate. It was typically used for bathing, but large enough to hold three or four adults. "Lower yourself down and let the water consume you."

"I do this to fulfill the will of my Father," said Christ. "I do this to save the lives of my apostles. Amen, amen I say to you blessed are those who believe in my Father's divine power and mercy, for yours will be the kingdom of God."

The two guards, the two priests, and Pilate then watched as the son of God disrobed His clothing, and gently placed Himself in the center of the pool, with His arms raised. Jesus then knelt and uttered His final word before allowing the water to fill His lungs and stop the beating of His heart.

After an hour, Pilate told the chief priests to go back home.

"There is nothing more for you here," said Pilate. "He is clearly dead."

"Tomorrow we will return to claim the body and show His followers how wrong they were about Him," said Annas.

"You can return around dusk and share a meal with myself and my wife, so that we can make those arrangements properly," said Pilate.

"As you wish, governor," said Annas.

There was still something though that was bothering Pilate.

"What was it that He said before he drowned Himself?" asked the governor. "I could not hear it."

"I did not hear it either," said Caiaphas.

"Nor did I," Annas said.

"Perhaps you did," Pilate said, pointing at the guard closest to the pool. "Did you?"

"Yes," he said. "I heard it clearly."

"Well, what was it?" Pilate was getting annoyed. "What was the word?"

"Abba."

Day 36: 1:30 a.m., Jerusalem, Upper Room

As John approached the apostles hiding place, he was wondering how he would be able to wake them up to gain entry. Fortunately, his brother spotted him on the street. James was on watch, monitoring the streets from the second floor vantage point.

"Good to see you, my brother," said James as he let John into the dark and musty upper room. The other nine men were all asleep scattered haphazardly about the floor. John was reluctant to wake them up at this hour, especially bearing such bad news.

"What brings you here at this hour?" asked James. "I thought you were in Nazareth with Mary."

"Jesus asked me to accompany Him to Jerusalem," John explained.

"The master is here within the city?"

"Yes, my brother. He is," said John. "That is what I have come to tell you about."

"I do not understand," said James. "Why did the master not come with you?"

By now several of the apostles had started to wake up, despite the best efforts of the two brothers to keep their voices down. This was not what John wanted to happen, to have to explain this to the entire group at once, because they might turn on him, and blame him for what happened.

"What is going on here?" asked Andrew, slowing sitting up and rubbing the sleep from his eyes. "Who is here, James?"

"It is John. He has returned from Nazareth with the master."

"Jesus is here?" Simon Peter was the next to wake up.

"No Peter, he is not," said John.

"Then where is He?" asked Matthew. All of the apostles were now standing up. Jude lit a lamp and brought it to the center of the room as the men gathered in a circle around John. The situation was getting tense. Being the youngest, John had sometimes felt a little intimidated and out of place by these men who in some cases were 20 years older than him. He did not know how to begin to tell them what happened, so he thought it might be best to begin with good news.

"Peter, the master tells me that you and Andrew have been ordered by the Sanhedrin to appear in front of them and Pilate later this day," said John.

"That is true," replied Peter. "We have been discussing what to do about this for days."

"The master has instructed me to tell you that you and Andrew are not to appear in front of the council. There will be no need for you to do so," said John.

"If we do not appear they will kill us, and they will probably kill the rest of us too, including you," said Andrew.

"You do not understand," said John.

"What do we not understand?" asked Peter. "What are you not telling us?"

There was a long pause. For a moment John did not think he could go on. His face turned red hot and then wet. He realized that tears were coursing down his burning cheeks.

"All of you need to realize is that this is not my fault," said John. "He chose to do this. This is the will of the Father."

"You need to tell us right now what has happened to Jesus," said Matthew, his voice rising in anger.

John closed his eyes, swallowed hard, and collapsed on the floor. Immediately James rushed over to him.

"Bring me the water basin and a rag," James said. His brother then began placing the cool towel on John's forehead to revive him.

"All of you back away," he said. "Give him some space."

James then lifted his younger brother up into his arms, and carried him to the open window to allow him to get some fresh air. Several minutes passed before John regained his composure.

"I feel better now," said John. "Thank you. I am ready to say what has happened on this horrible night."

The rest of the men then began to make their way towards the window where John was now sitting.

"Jesus has been arrested again," John said.

"Surely this cannot be true," said Simon.

"Who has done this to him?" said Andrew. "How could He allow this to happen?"

"The Sanhedrin and Pilate have him in custody," said John.

"What will happen to him?" asked Peter.

"It is likely that He will be killed," said John. "In fact, He is probably already dead."

The men started to scream. Some fell to their knees, and pulled on their hair. Others just stood in disbelief.

"This is all my fault," said Simon Peter. "He is doing this to spare my life."

"No," said Matthew. "He is doing this to spare all of our lives."

"I cannot bare to think of the suffering He at this hour is going through because of me," said Peter. "Did he say that he shall return?"

"No, he did not," said John. "He seemed unsure of His Father's will, only that he must carry it out no matter what happened to him. He wants to die to protect us."

"If they kill Jesus again," said Peter, "all that tells me is that we going to be next. I have tried to follow Jesus but it has lead to nothing but disaster. Now he is probably dead again, with no hope for His return, and the Jews will likely come for us next. What hope is there if the master is now gone? I have no will to continue without Him. I feel as if He has abandoned us. I feel nothing but fear, hopelessness, and guilt."

"What are you going to do, Peter?" asked Andrew.

"I am going back home to Galilee. I am giving up. There is

nothing more for me here but death and fear," he said. "I am going fishing."

"You are making a mistake," said Matthew. "You need to have faith."

"I agree," said Jude. "Jesus is testing us. We gave up on Him when He died the first time, hiding out here like cowards. Now he has given his life for us again and you do nothing but betray him again."

"I agree with Jude," said Simon. "And James feels the same way."

"Then the four of us will not go with you," said Matthew. "We will remain here."

"I admire your faith Matthew," said Peter. "But my soul is crushed with guilt and fear. You are a better man than I am, but this is my decision. I want to be with my family. I am done. I want to go home where it is safe and where I can live my life free of fear and sadness. My guilt is too much to overcome right now to stay with you here in this city that has taken everything from me over and over again. I blame myself for what has happened. When will it end? He is dead and not coming back. We have to accept this."

"So be it," said Matthew. "I know your mind is made up."

Andrew, Thomas, Nathanael, James, John, and Philip agreed to go with Peter back to Bethsaida. Preparations for the three day journey were made immediately. After a few more hours of sleep, the seven men set out for Galilee not knowing when if ever they would return to the holy city.

Day 37: 6 p.m., Jerusalem, home of Pontius Pilate

During the night the pool that contained the lifeless body of the son of God was being surreptitiously watched by a curious set of eyes. Besides the two Roman guards, a certain figure crept in the shadows. She stayed behind the pillars with a watchful eye for any movement of the still water that lay blanketing the Nazarene.

Claudia first saw Him in her sleep. To call them dreams would not convey the immediacy of those visions. Jesus had spoken to her directly, and all that she could feel was the love of God filling her soul as nothing had touched her before. When she found out that her husband had executed this innocent man the dreams turned to nightmares as she could see and feel His suffering.

Now he had suffered again for reasons that she could not understand. Her husband assured her that this time Jesus willingly submitted Himself to this death, and that she should not hope for his return. This may be how he intended to peacefully bring his life to an end to save the life of his friends. Despite the protestations of Pilate, she remained vigilant, hoping to witness His return from the dead.

What she did witness though was difficult to describe when she would look back on this day years later. This moment changed her life, and made her into a follower of Christ. All that she could initially recall was the abundance of light that surrounded Jesus as He rose from that basin. All of the water that surrounded Him was now gone as his body was transfixed by light. The atmosphere around her had shifted. Time and space were just concepts that she once knew the meaning of, but had no relevance to what she was seeing with her eyes. The Nazarene then began moving towards her. Claudia prostrated herself on the ground. She looked up and reached her hand out to Jesus.

"Do not touch me for I have not ascended to my Father."

Claudia recoiled in fear. "They call you teacher," she said. "Yet I am but a lowly sinner."

"Follow me, and sin no more," said Jesus. "Your mind will now be at peace."

She knew that the nightmares would now come to an end with this gift of peace.

The two Roman guards then walked over to Jesus. Both of them kneeled in front of Him, and then laid down their swords and shields at His feet.

"We serve only you, my Lord. We will honor and protect you all the days of our lives, for truly you are the son of God."

"Peace be with you. One day you will be soldiers for my Father in paradise. Bring me to see the governor."

The four of them then proceeded to walk towards the dining hall, where Pilate had just sat down with Annas and Caiaphas to begin the first course of their evening meal. Claudia insisted on going into the room first, followed by the guards. Jesus told her that He could not enter the room unless He was invited in by Pilate, so this had to be the order of events.

"We were just looking for you," said Pilate to Claudia. "Will you be joining us?"

"No, there are more important matters to discuss," she said.

"Like the Nazarene," said Annas.

"Yes," Claudia said. "You are here to collect His body and prove that you were right to execute Him, are you not?"

"Yes," said Caiaphas. "That is why we are here."

"Your lack of faith will be your ultimate demise," she said.

At that moment the two guards who witnessed Jesus' resurrection just minutes ago entered the room. Pilate angrily stood up from his chair.

"What is the meaning of this intrusion?" he said. "Where are your swords and shields?"

"We no longer serve you, or Caesar. We are disciples of the living Christ and the kingdom of God the Father."

"Your living Christ is dead," said Annas.

Pilate could sense something different in his wife. He found himself needing to sit back down, and quiet his rage.

"The Nazarene is alive." The words were supposed to be a question, but came out as a statement of fact. Pilate knew it to be true. He could see the peace in her eyes that had not been there in months, if not years.

"Jesus, son of God," said Pilate. "Show yourself to us."

The messiah then entered the chamber, as the chief priests

gasped, and recoiled in their chairs.

"Peace be with you," said Jesus. "My Father's will has been done for you to witness."

"Surely this is some trick," said Caiaphas.

"You know as well as I do that He was dead," Pilate angrily shot back at him.

"We stood guard day and night, alternating shifts, watching his lifeless body remain as such hour after hour," said the older guard. "This man was dead. We will testify to this."

Pilate slowly approached Jesus and smiled at him.

"My God will always be Caesar. It is too late for me. I do not know what you are, or who you are, but I am not a foolish man," said Pilate. "I see nothing but disaster if I attempt to arrest and execute your followers. This would cause nothing but more disorder, and create further anguish, both of which would make it harder for me to rule. I have seen with my eyes your power. Who am I to stand in your way?"

By now, the chief priests had left, without saying anything further to Pilate. Whether it was fear, anger, or disbelief that drove them from that room it was unclear. Pilate did make note of their rapid exit.

"I cannot speak to how they are going to react to this," said Pilate. "I am not Jewish, but I imagine they will still view you and your followers as a threat to their power. As long as I remain as governor here, none of your men will be executed under Roman law here in Jerusalem. I cannot say as much for the Sanhedrin."

"Then we will just have to have faith," said Jesus. "I have witnessed it myself here today."

Jesus knew that long after he was gone, there would be a constant unseen force guiding Pilate in the right direction. His wife, Claudia.

Day 40: 6 a.m., Sea of Tiberius

The journey from Jerusalem had been a somber affair. There was little conversation between the men, mostly discussions of where to sleep and get food. There was no point in casting blame or arguing about what had happened. Each step seemed to fortify their will to keep moving forward. Each step would put their former lives that much further in the past. Peter wondered if the boats would even be usable three years later. He had left instructions to the hired help to maintain the fishing business as best they could, but at this point it was anyone's guess whether the fishing boats would be abandoned, or in complete disrepair. Much to his relief, upon reaching Bethsaida, Peter and Andrew found that the boats had been well taken care for, so much so that all seven men could resume fishing that very night.

Everyone agreed that it was therapeutic to ease back into the old, familiar ways in the water they had fished in since they were boys with their fathers. It was surprising then that hour after hour they caught nothing. Peter was growing increasingly frustrated with the lack of any results, and was almost ready to order the boats in for the day. Dawn was breaking, and they could just as well try this again tomorrow. It had been a long journey. The air was vacant, and the water softly lapping off the sides of the boats. Earlier, Peter had instructed the men to stay quiet so he grew annoyed when he heard a voice from the shore mocking his futile efforts.

"Children, have you caught anything to eat?"

"No!" Peter yelled back at the intruder.

"Cast the net over the right side of the boat and you will find something."

Thinking he would like nothing better than to prove this unwanted interloper wrong, Peter did as he was told. He cast the net, but much to his shock was unable to pull it in, due to the large number of fish. John immediately knew they had just witnessed a miracle.

"It is the Lord!" the beloved apostle said to Peter.

Peter immediately tucked in his garment and jumped into the sea, half swimming, half running towards Jesus in unfettered joy. His savior had returned from the dead. The apostles followed in their boats and came ashore as well, bringing with them 153 fish.

"Bring some of the fish you just caught," Jesus said. The master had prepared a charcoal fire with bread and fish on it. The men sat down and formed a circle around Jesus, as they prepared to share this final meal with Him, a sacred ritual among friends. The men hung their heads in shame, not daring to look at the man they betrayed. Jesus broke the bread and gave it to His disciples, and in a like manner, the fish.

"This is my body that I have given up for you, my friends."

When the men had finished eating breakfast, the attention turned to Peter. Jesus was clearly disappointed in the actions Simon Peter had taken in returning to Galilee.

"Simon, son of John, do you love me more than these?" Jesus said, gesturing to the nets, and the fishing rods. Peter could feel the shame and guilt building within him. He remembered how Jesus told him that he could no longer be a fisherman, but instead a fisher of men.

"Yes, Lord you know that I love you," Peter said.

"Feed my lambs," Jesus said.

"Simon, son of John, do you love me?"

"Yes, Lord, you know that I love you."

"Tend my sheep," Jesus said.

"Simon, son of John, do you love me?"

Peter began to cry and become severely distressed.

"Lord, you know everything," he said. "You know that I love you."

"Feed my sheep," Jesus said.

The master then smiled at Simon Peter, and sought to ease some of his anxiety.

"Amen, amen I say to you when you were younger, you used

to dress yourself and go where you wanted; but when you grow old, you will stretch out your hands, and someone else will dress you, and lead you to where you do not want to go."

Simon Peter liked hearing this rather humorous statement from the master. In his mind he no longer had to fear death with this assurance from Christ that he would die an old man.

"Follow me," Jesus said. "Remember that you are all fishers of men and have nothing to fear in building the kingdom of God."

Jesus then turned His attention to John. There were some things He had to discuss with the beloved apostle before leaving. Peter inquired after this, asking Jesus, "Lord, what about him?"

Jesus said to Peter, "What concern is it of yours? You follow me."

Jesus then said to John, "Please continue to take care of my mother, for today I ascend to my Father's kingdom."

"As you wish my Lord," said John. "Is it here that you will leave us?"

"No, my child," said Jesus. "I see that Simon, Jude, Matthew, and James are not here in Galilee."

"They chose to remain in Jerusalem," said John.

"Their faith was strong," said the Lord, "and it is because of this faith that they will witness my last moment on this earth."

Day 40: 6 p.m., Mount of Olives

As the days went by without any sign of the Lord, tensions began to mount among the four men. Staying in the upper room was beginning to be untenable given the paucity of the food supply. Matthew began to think that it might be best to do as Peter did, and return to his former life as a tax collector, so with that in mind he left the others the previous morning. The remaining three were not ready to give up all hope just yet.

"Let us pray as Jesus taught us," said Jude. "He said when two or more of you gather in my name, there I will be in your midst."

Jude, Simon, and James then formed a circle in the center of the room, linked their hands, and closed their eyes.

"Peace be with you, my friends."

The men all turned towards the door to see Jesus with his hands raised towards them.

"My Lord and my God," said James. "We have stayed vigilant and kept the faith."

"That faith has sustained you more than any bread," said Jesus. "Your courage has quenched your thirst more than any water. I am the bread of life. Your faith is why I am here."

"You have suffered so much for us my Lord," said Jude. "I have been tormented by the very thought of the continued suffering you have endured for the will of the Father."

"My suffering will now end, for today I return to my Father, and it is you who will witness the glory of my Ascension."

"Where will this take place, my Lord?" asked James.

"Where I have always felt closest to my Father," said Jesus. "We will go to Gethsemane and then ascend the Mount of Olives. Come, my friends. The time is at hand."

When they reached the Mount of Olives, Jesus was strangely quiet for almost an hour, kneeling in prayer, facing away from the other men. Simon could occasionally hear the master murmur a word or two, but most of what He was saying was incoherent. When Christ rose to His feet, he turned to the men and began to smile.

"It is time for me to return to my Father," said Jesus. "His will has been done. Your faith has led you here."

"Jesus, how can we continue without you?" said James. "We are afraid for our lives."

"There is nothing to fear. All the power in heaven and earth has been given to me," said the master. "Go therefore and make disciples of all nations, baptizing them in the name of the Father, and of the Son, and of the Holy Spirit. Teach them to observe all that I have commanded you."

The three men then kneeled in front of their savior.

"Close your eyes, my children," said Jesus, who then proceeded to lay his hands on each of their heads. "Behold I am with you always, until the end of the age."

When Jude, James, and Simon opened their eyes it seemed as if hours had passed. They found themselves lying on the ground, as if waking from a deep sleep. Jesus was gone.

"We have much work to do," said James.

"Yes, we need to summon Peter and bring all of the apostles back to Jerusalem," said Jude.

"I could not hear what the master was saying while he was praying," said James.

"I could not understand it either," said Jude. "You were closest to him. Did you hear what he was praying, Simon?"

"I only heard one word distinctly that He repeated many times," said Simon.

"Well, what was it?" James asked. "What did the master say?"

"Abba."

Endnotes

1.   http://www.creeds.net/ancient/nicene.htm. "He has spoken through the prophets."
2.   http://www.creeds.net/ancient/nicene.htm. "For our sake He was crucified under Pontius Pilate."
3.   http://www.religioustolerance.org/gospj3.htm
4.   http://www.jcrelations.net/Klassen%2C+William.+Judas %3A+Betrayer+or+Friend+of+Jesus%3F.2565.0.html?L=3
5.   The New American Bible, (Wichita, Kansas: Catholic Bible Publishers, 1991), 1055.
6.   http://www.britannica.com/EBchecked/topic/307411/Judas-Iscariot
7.   http://www3.telus.net/trbrooks/12groups.htm
8.   TNAB, 1246.
9.   Ibid., 1062.
10. Ibid., 1061.
11. http://www.biography.com/people/pontius-pilate-9440686# prefect-of-judea
12. Philo, On The Embassy of Gauis Book XXXVIII 299–305.
13. Josephus, Antiquities of the Jews 18.3.2
14. http://www.jewishvirtuallibrary.org/jsource/judaica/ejud_ 0002_0007_0_07198.html
15. TNAB, 1173.
16. Ibid., 1175
17. Ibid., 1180.
18. http://www.britannica.com/EBchecked/topic/305163/Saint-John-the-Apostle
19. TNAB, 1180.
20. Ibid., 1181.
21. http://www.biography.com/people/pontius-pilate-9440686#prefect-of-judea
22. https://www.biblegateway.com/resources/all-women-bible/

Pilate-8217-s-Wife

23. http://www.creeds.net/ancient/nicenel.htm. "On the third day He rose again." Does the word "again" here imply a second resurrection?

24. Ibid., 1166.

25. Ibid.

26. Ibid., 1167

27. Ibid.

28. Edwyn Hoskyns, The Fourth Gospel, (London: Faber and Faber Limited, 1947), 544-545.

29. http://dhspriory.org/thomas/John20.htm

30. TNAB, 1167

31. Ibid.

32. http://www.ushistory.org/Paine/crisis/c-01.htm

33. TNAB, 1168

34. Ibid.

35. http://www.agapebiblestudy.com/john_gospel/Introduction .htm

36. Ibid.

37. TNAB, 1167.

38. Ibid., 1393.

39. Ibid., 1158.

40. Ibid., 1165.

41. Ibid., 1166.

42. http://www.agapebiblestudy.com/john_gospel/Introduction .htm

43. TNAB, 1168.

44. Ibid., 1150.

45. Ibid., 1152.

46. Ibid., 1156.

47. Hoskyns, 554.

48. Ibid., 555.

49. Raymond E. Brown, The Gospel According to John, (Garden City, New York: Doubleday, 1970), 1080.

50. http://www.creeds.net/ancient/nicenel.htm. "We look for the resurrection of the dead."
51. TNAB, 1143
52. Ibid., 1145.
53. Ibid., 1147.
54. Ibid., 1140.
55. Ibid., 1168.
56. Ibid., 1138.
57. Ibid., 1143.
58. http://www.merriam-webster.com/dictionary/apostasy
59. TNAB, 1156.
60. Ibid.
61. Hoskyns, 552.
62. Brown, 1069.
63. TNAB, 1170.
64. http://www.bibleinfo.com/en/questions/who-were-twelve-disciples.
65. Ibid.
66. bid.
67. Ibid.
68. Ibid.
69. Ibid., 1167.
70. Ibid.
71. Ibid..
72. Ibid., 1168.
73. Ibid., 1167.
74. https://www.google.com/#q=what+does+acrostic+mean
75. http://www.religionfacts.com/christianity/symbols/fish.htm
76. http://www.christianitytoday.com/ch/asktheexpert/oct26.html
77. https://translate.google.com/#auto/la/first%20breakfast
78. TNAB., 1168.
79. Ibid.
80. Ibid.

81. Ibid.
82. Ibid.
83. Ibid.
84. Ibid.
85. Ibid.
86. Ibid., 1171.
87. Ibid., 1166.
88. Ibid., 1167.
89. Ibid., 1170.
90. Ibid., 1066.
91. Ibid., 1134.
92. http://www.bibleplaces.com/mtolives.htm
93. https://www.google.com/maps/dir/JesusBoat,+Ginosar
94. TNAB, 1171.
95. http://www.bibleinfo.com/en/questions/who-were-twelve-disciples
96. http://prophecytracker.org/2014/04/passover-begins-at-sundown-tonight/
97. http://www.ctlibrary.com/ch/1998/issue59/59h028.html
98. TNAB, 1138.
99. Ibid., 1141.
100. Ibid., 1143.
101. Ibid., 1144.
102. Ibid., 1148.
103. Ibid., 1163.

Chronos Books is a historical non-fiction imprint. Chronos publishes real history for real people; bringing to life historical people, places and events in an imaginative, easy-to-digest and accessible way. We want writers of historical books, from ancient times to the Second World War, that will add to our understanding of people and events rather than being a dry textbook; history that passes on its stories to a generation of new readers.